Revised & Updated

Grace ON TRIAL

The Heartwarming Message
the Lord "Sent" to Us in 1888

Robert J. Wieland

Glad Tidings Publishers
8784 Valley View Drive
Berrien Springs, MI U.S.A.

Grace ON TRIAL
The Heartwarming Message the Lord "Sent" to Us in 1888

Robert J. Wieland
Copyright © 2001 by Robert J. Wieland

Originally accepted by Pacific Press for publication and titled by them, *Grace on Trial,* and published by the 1888 Message Study Committee, August 1988 (10,000 copies). Second printing, October 1988 (10,000 copies). Printings also in Russian and French.

Revised and updated, 2001.

Unless otherwise indicated, Scripture is taken from the New King James Version.
Bible texts credited to KJV are from the King James Version.
Bible texts credited to NEB are from the New English Bible.
Bible texts credited to NIV are from the New International Version.
Bible texts credited to TEV are from the Good News Bible, the Bible in Today's English Version.

Book and cover design by Nova Artworks.

ISBN 1-931218-55-2

[00116]

Contents

Dedication

To Grace, My Wife

*Whose love, fidelity, patience,
and innumerable goodnesses
have made my pathway a happy one.*

Preface

The editors of a major North American Seventh-day Adventist Publishing House asked the author to write the manuscript for this book. Their plan was to publish it in time for the Centennial camp-meeting season and Centennial celebration in Minneapolis.

In due course their reading committee and the editors enthusiastically accepted the manuscript, proceeding to process it for publication. Due to circumstances beyond their control, they were forced to drop its publication. The General Conference were pursuing a different philosophy.

Glad Tidings Publishers present this book to the Seventh-day Adventist Church. An edited version (*Powerful Good News*) minus references to Ellen White, Jones, and Waggoner, is also presented to the world. There are ordained ministers and loyal lay members who believe that "the most precious message" which the Lord sent to the Seventh-day Adventist Church over a century ago needs to be widely understood today in its authentic form.

They also look forward to the time when this church shall be united in a joyful acceptance of the message which Ellen White endorsed so highly. It will yet lighten the earth with the glory of a much more abounding grace that is no longer frustrated or put "on trial" within the remnant church itself. A growing phenomenal worldwide interest in that message indicates that the Holy Spirit is renewing the opportunities that were ours over a century ago.

All non-biblical footnote references not otherwise credited are from Ellen G. White sources.

WHEN HEAVEN CAUGHT "US" BY SURPRISE

Seventh-day Adventists worldwide have cherished a favorite conviction: that the second coming of Christ is near. But they also realize that two immense events must happen *before He can return:*

(1) The heavenly gift of the "latter rain" must be sent from God and then be *accepted* by the church in order to prepare a people for the next event:

(2) The "loud cry" of the final message must "lighten the earth with glory." On God's agenda, this alone can catalyze humanity into two groups—those who receive the final "seal of God" and those who receive "the mark of the beast."

Because the Father still loves the world for whom He gave His only begotten Son, a message of much more abounding grace must be the "voice from heaven" that the apostle John heard will sound everywhere.[1] God knows it wouldn't be fair for Jesus to come before everyone could hear the message of grace clearly proclaimed. The confusion of Babylon must be resolved in people's minds. That final message must therefore be a clearer understanding of true righteousness by faith.

A growing number of Seventh-day Adventists worldwide are coming to see how both of these grand events coalesced in a little known event that happened over a century ago: God sent us what is known as "the 1888 message." Our fascination with it now spans three centuries of Seventh-day Adventist existence.

Why Does the Interest Persist?

A gravitational pull lures us to this momentous event, rivaling 1844 in our corporate memory. Even a Centennial Celebration in 1988 could not bury the controversies swirling around what happened (or what didn't happen). That strange date still magnetizes us even in this new century. A General Conference session with less than 100 delegates in a humble little wooden church—shouldn't the story be buried in our attic dust? Why can't we forget it?

Could it be that God Himself won't let us? An image of past history intrudes itself into current history. For example, at the 1893 General Conference Session, the tension of "Minneapolis" excitement permeated the *Daily Bulletins.* It also formed the backdrop of the great 1901 Session, impressing speakers and delegates alike. Until her death in 1915, Ellen White kept pleading for the recovery of the spiritual experience that she often said eluded us in 1888 and afterwards.

After her death, throughout the 1920s "1888" surfaced repeatedly in our denominational consciousness, dominating *Review* articles, Weeks of Prayer, and sermons at Conference ministers' meetings. Testimonials and reminiscences of the few who had attended the 1888 session were collected. No other event in our church's history seems to have motivated such a search for rare eyewitness accounts.

The 1950s saw a crescendo of concern. The unprecedented 1952 Bible Conference claimed the 1888 message as the supreme topic of "practically every speaker from the first day onward, … spontaneous." The General Conference president even said that the message had been preached more powerfully than it was in 1888.[2]

Now in our day the keen interest continues. Our denominational publishing houses still pursue it, producing tome after tome trying to satisfy worldwide curiosity about a strange "most precious message" that has assumed a legendary mystique.

Is there a reason why that small gathering in Minneapolis in the fall of 1888 has held a spotlight focus on our denominational stage?

Does God Keep Bringing the Subject Up?

Something has invested "1888" with its compulsive interest. Even if sinful time were to go on for a thousand years (Heaven forbid!), God's Spirit would keep that memory alive for an important reason: "1888" was a divine confrontation with His people that can never be forgotten: *it rivals Pentecost in significance.*

This is because an eschatological crisis was looming beyond the humble event itself. We sense that the key to solving our denominational lukewarmness will be found only there. Even the seemingly never-ending controversies that swirl around the history presage an ultimate solution. Mystery cannot forever prevail.

Seventh-day Adventist historians have described the 1888 Conference as "epochal ... [standing] out like a mountain peak," "the most crucial of all our General Conferences," "a notable landmark in Seventh-day Adventist history ... like crossing a continental divide into a new country," "a providence designed to initiate the beginning of a new era," "a new depiction of Christ delineated by dedicated new draftsmen." "Minneapolis" and "1888" "go together in Adventist history like husband and wife."[3]

A Second-Coming Experimental Test Case

The delegates at this leadership session came unexpectedly face to face with Jesus as our High Priest, and they were not prepared for the encounter. It was a fulfillment of an ancient prophecy, "The Lord, whom you seek, will suddenly come to His temple, ... [but] who can abide the day of His coming?"[4]

Of course, it was not a literal second coming; it was a divinely appointed test. Ellen White says that Christ revealed Himself in a message and in two specially "delegated messengers."[5] He loves His people too much to appear in a literal second coming "in the glory of His power" before they are prepared, for they couldn't stand a personal confrontation; His brightness would "slay" them.[6] They must experience a special heart preparation in order to endure His physical presence when He finally comes "in the clouds." In mercy therefore He must first reveal Himself in a "special message" of righteousness. Their reaction to that message would determine what would happen if He were to appear in glory literally.

The History of the Jews Re-visited

In numerous clear-cut statements Ellen White discloses that a rare fulfillment of Bible prophecy occurred at that small gathering. For the most part, the delegates were unaware of it, as the people of Bethlehem were unaware of what happened in the stable the night Christ was born.

According to her prophetic insight, Heaven came near to impart a blessing unprecedented since Pentecost. *It was the "beginning" of the loud cry of Revelation 18, and it had to be also the beginning of the latter rain.*[7]

The initial *early rain* of the Holy Spirit launched the world gospel evangel. According to Ellen White, "1888" marked the "beginning" of the *final* outpouring of the same Holy Spirit—for the completion of that world mission.[8] Thus Pentecost and "1888" are linked by a common divine purpose. The Lord intended the Minneapolis Conference to be the launching of the last phase of the world movement pictured in Revelation 18—to lighten the earth with the glory of the fourth angel's message of much more abounding grace.[9]

How could a stupendous event like that take place in such a humble gathering? Something as far-reaching as a complement to Pentecost deserves a more auspicious debut! Why didn't the Holy Spirit wait until we could meet in one of our glittering sessions on a spot-lighted stage in a vast arena seating 100,000 people? A splendid modern General Conference session convening in one of the world's great cities would give the loud cry message a proper sendoff.

Why the Humble Circumstance of That Event?

One reason is the personality of the Lord Jesus. He apparently didn't want to wait; should He not be eager to return to claim His bride? He sensed that the time for "the marriage of the Lamb has come" (Revelation 19:7). His love was real. He had promised concerning those who saw the first signs of the "time of the end" that "this generation shall not pass, till all these things be fulfilled." The time had come for the finishing of the work of God, and Jesus, still human as well as divine, was eager for it. It was to be the holy trysting place, the betrothal dramatized in the Song of Solomon. The message which He "sent" was to do its work and prepare *that generation* to meet Him at His literal second coming. The message itself was to be the means of "the Bride [making] herself ready."

The Convergence of a Unique National Event

Even American national history demonstrated how a ferment of the human spirit demanded that Heaven's final message of grace be sounded quickly. Roman Catholicism and Protestantism in general were being alerted to hear the message, some to accept joyfully, others to oppose conclusively. The American Congress has never yet come so close to passing a national Sunday law as during the era of Senator H. W. Blair and his proposed religious legislation.[10] The climax that all Christians wait for was nearer then than many think it is now. Other nations would have been ready to follow the American lead in fulfillment of the Revelation 13:11-16 prophecy of religious persecution. The dragon was ready to roar.

The two young messengers who brought the message to the Minneapolis Conference were instrumental in opposing intolerant legislation that almost passed the American Congress. Clergymen were thirsting to violate the principle of the First Constitutional Amendment by demanding that Congress pass national religious legislation in a Sunday law.

Americans are indebted to those two obscure messengers for this continuing century and more of religious liberty. If people only knew, they would erect a statute to them on the Mall. A national Sunday law in violation of the American Constitution would have opened floodgates of intolerance and consequent failure of the American dream of liberty and prosperity. A national crisis was looming.

But there was more involved than religious politics. No one can read our history and doubt that God has entrusted to this people His last message of grace for the world. It was ordained to supply a final cure for the problem of deep-rooted sin, producing a beautiful change in believing humanity, evidence that the sacrifice of Christ was not in vain. He defeated Satan at the cross, but now He must be glorified in His people. Satan's accusations must be forever silenced.

The "most precious message" the Lord sent us was more than a thunder-and-lightning denunciation of sin abounding; it was a heart-warming revelation of grace *much more* abounding, a final reconciliation of alienated human hearts to God and to His holy law. It would capture the full devotion of every honest heart worldwide. The righteousness Christ accomplished in Himself would be displayed again in a generation of people who would "follow the Lamb whithersoever He goeth."[11]

How the Message can be Misunderstood Today

The problem is that the popular Sunday-keeping churches also have their version of "righteousness by faith" which since then has infiltrated Seventh-day Adventist thinking. In our human minds without our realizing what has happened, it can replace the essential elements of the unique "most precious message" heaven "sent" to us.

The message that God "sent" was healing balm for the sickness of soul that the old covenant produces. Throughout our decades we have been obsessed with the deeply rooted old covenant idea that "we-must-do-this," "we-must-do-that," "we-must-be-more-faithful," "we-must-get-the-victory," "we-must-study-more," "we-must-pray-more,""we-must-witness more,""musts" almost *ad infinitum*. As it was millennia ago, many ask with the Jews,"What shall we *do* that we might work the works of God?" There can be a real but latent fear of something too good to be true—salvation by grace alone; our program of doing "obedience" might appear to suffer.

A fear of being lost is the bottom line because faith is not understood as a heart-appreciation of the heavenly love that casts out fear.[12] Hungry souls and discouraged hearts are the fruit of an old covenant mindset.

The Result?

A thermostatic spiritual "balance" that is called "lukewarmness." A widespread spiritual illness testifies to a confusion about the message of Christ's righteousness. Enthusiastic new converts come in and after a few years for the most part imbibe the same spiritual illness, like an infusion of good blood soon becomes infected also. Even intense activity in "missionary work" is not the cure-all.

The reason Ellen White was overjoyed with the 1888 message was because it revealed a salvation by grace alone that is received through a *faith which works*. It was not legalism, but it produced real obedience to the law of God. She saw how proclaiming this unique justification by faith would lead people to accept the full message, including that of the Sabbath. For the first time here was a message that transcended fear and truly cast it out. And it would have finished the gospel commission because it broke through the fog, replacing legalistic imperatives with gospel enablings. Spiritual power was implicit within the message itself; but like electricity from the power plant it awaited a switch-on in order to complete the circuit.

The Lord meant that the message should go triumphantly to the world through a revelation of His grace in the "third angel's message in verity," which Ellen White said was the unique 1888 idea of justification by faith. Because of our humble numbers and lowly world image, the glory would all go to God. A message, not denominational pride, would be honored.

It would lighten the earth before the horrors of World Wars I and II, before walls should isolate billions from hearing it, and before the tragic disintegration of the social fabric that has corrupted the world in the last century. Through drug abuse, debauchery and disease, millions now seem beyond the capacity even to hear or understand the last-days "everlasting gospel." And millions more are now either ill with HIV, have died of AIDS while still young, or are locked in emotional terror of it.

Why the Message Was Such a Surprise When It Came

Another reason for the suddenness of the 1888 encounter is that God's way of doing things always catches us unexpectedly. He seems to have an out-sized sense of humor. Think of letting His Messiah be born at Bethlehem in a stinking stable with cows and goats instead of in Caesar's or at least the high priest's palace. No one would offer Him a room. Seldom if ever has any fresh intervention from heaven been recognized and acclaimed when first disclosed. God's messengers have repeatedly been forced to "prophesy in sackcloth."

Our 1888 history is the same general story, with a significant innovation. What makes it different is this: for the first time Seventh-day Adventist *ministers and leaders* joined the innkeeper at Bethlehem in saying to Jesus, "No room here!"

According to the little lady who discerned motivations that others did not readily perceive, our delegates did even worse. In scorning God's "special messengers" whom He sent, Ellen White says over a hundred times that they rivaled the Jewish rulers in shamefully treating Christ.[13] Unbelievable as it may appear, she adds that the bulk of them actually "insulted the Holy Spirit."[14]

And whereas the apostles eagerly accepted and welcomed the initial *early rain* outpouring of the Holy Spirit at Pentecost, most of "us" (in a corporate sense) felt compelled to resist the beginning of the final *latter rain* outpouring of the same Holy Spirit.[15] It's a painful story to tell; and that of the Jews' rejection of Christ is also painful to tell. But truth cannot be evaded, for the gospel is involved in history.

Heaven Was Astonished

What happened surprised the angels, while at the same time "the disappointment" of the Lord Jesus "was beyond description."[16] (In chapters to follow, we shall let Ellen White have her documented say.) The 1888 Conference and its aftermath for about a decade stands out in heroic proportions because of two complementary, contrasting dimensions in the event: unprecedented blessings in the message itself, inspired by the Holy Spirit; and unprecedented opposition against it inspired by His opponent:

(1) The message of grace was unique in its pristine New Testament purity, a recovery of truth unprecedented since apostolic times, a message intended to carry the sixteenth-century Reformation to greater heights than Luther or even the Wesleys could anticipate. (The support for this is the simple fact that the message was the "beginning" of the final loud cry of Revelation 18 which is not noise but light.)[17]

(2) The reaction of our brethren to the message was likewise unique in the nature of its opposition. Never before had Seventh-day Adventist ministers and leaders formed a phalanx of resistance to Ellen White. She said at the time, "We have had the hardest and most incomprehensible tug of war we have ever had among our people. ... My testimony has made the least impression upon many minds than at any period before in my history."[18] "I was never more alarmed than at the present time."[19]

It's true that as long as sin and Satan exist there is bound to be conflict between darkness and light, falsehood and truth. And yes, since its inception in the early nineteenth century, the Advent movement has realized that "the dragon was wroth with the woman, and went to make war with the remnant of her seed, which keep the commandments of God, and have the testimony of Jesus Christ."[20] Our pioneers had to meet that opposition from sources both outside and inside the church. So what's new?

Something significant: the dragon's opposition took a new turn. Now his voice found echoes inside *the leadership* of the remnant church, who sincerely, honestly did not discern what was going on.

Why the "1888" Story is Arresting and Sobering

Like ancient Bethlehem that was "little among the thousands of Judah," the Seventh-day Adventist Church was "little" among the many millions of Christian people in hundreds of denominations in the world. In only one way can we understand why God should honor a humble gathering of our delegates with "the beginning" of the long-awaited latter rain, the final "Pentecost." It was not because this church is any more worthy than others, but it is the story of Israel repeated. The Lord was true to His ancient people, not because they were more deserving than other nations, but because of His honor in the divine election of Abraham's descendants. Many were shamefully unworthy, but God's loyalty endured. Heaven is involved in a similar crisis of identity with Seventh-day Adventist history.

The Seventh-day Adventist Church was raised up as a fulfillment of prophecy and thus has a special divine mandate. But because of that singular honor, God had the right to confront her with a solemn call to discharge her responsibility, and to confer on her the means of grace to succeed. Therein appears the double significance of "1888."

Has Heaven Backed Off From the Issues?

The story is closely interwoven with Christ's last message to "the angel of the church of the Laodiceans." In that light it makes sense.[21] With deep reverence we can wonder if by now Christ may be tempted to impatience. Surely, we are told, the angels *are* impatient.

He shares all the pain of earth's suffering millions, for "in all their affliction He [is] afflicted."[22] He cannot abandon a world that has never heard "the third angel's message *in verity,*" its special validation of grace much more abounding. There are too many suffering and yearning humans crying in anguish, "Please, Heaven, hear us." They need a message, and it was entrusted to us. How can we balance God's love for a world with His indulgence of our spiritual lethargy?

Our radio, TV, and satellite evangelism has never been more widespread than today. Multitudes are flowing into the church.

But has that special message become passé that Jesus sends to the last of the seven churches?

Here joins the issue.

Chapter One Endnotes

[1] Revelation 18:1-4.

[2] William H. Branson, in *Our Firm Foundation,* Vol. 2, p. 616 (the General Conference president). Analysis of the printed messages in the two-volume set reveals that the essentially unique 1888 concepts seldom got through. Acceptance of the 1952 message was virtually total; if it was indeed a revival of the latter rain and the loud cry (as he claimed), would not the gospel commission have been completed in that generation? There was no opposition. The only answer is that which motif analysis demonstrates: there was not a revival of the 1888 message content.

[3] Cf. L. E. Froom, *Movement of Destiny,* p. 187; A. W. Spalding, *Captains of the Host,* pp. 583, 602; L. H. Christian, *The Fruitage of Spiritual Gifts,* pp. 244, 245; A. G. Daniells, *Christ Our Righteousness,* p. 56; Mervyn Maxwell, *Tell It to the World,* p. 232.

[4] Malachi 3:1.

[5] *Testimonies to Ministers,* p. 97.

[6] 2 Thessalonians 1:8, 9.

[7] The angel informed Ellen White that the latter rain prepares the church to proclaim the loud cry message and must therefore precede it (*Early Writings,* p. 271). She also identified the 1888 message as initial "showers from heaven of the latter rain" (*Special Testimonies,* Series A, No. 6, p. 19).

[8] Cf. *Review and Herald,* March 22, November 22, 29, 1892; *General Conference Bulletin,*1893, pp. 38, 39, 243, 377, 463.

[9] Letter B2a, 1892; *Selected Messages,* Book 1, pp. 234, 235.

[10] Cf. *Seventh-day Adventist Encyclopedia,* p. 1273.

[11] Cf. Romans 8:4; Revelation 19:8. In both texts "righteousness" is the Greek *dikaiomata.* Always, *dikaiosune* is Christ's righteousness; *dikaiomata* is translated "the righteousness of saints." It is Christ's *dikaiosune* "fulfilled" in them.

[12] Cf. 1 John 4:17-19.

[13] Cf. MSS 9, 15, 1888; *Through Crisis to Victory,* pp. 292, 297, 300; MS 13, 1889; *Review and Herald,* March 4, 11, August 26, 1890; April 11, 18, 1893; *Testimonies to Ministers,* pp. 64, 75-80.

[14] Cf. MS 9, 1888; Olson op. cit., pp. 290, 291; MS 30, 1889; Letter S24, 1892; *Testimonies to Ministers,* p. 393.

[15] The White Estate have compiled 1821 pages of Ellen White testimony about the 1888 message and its history wherein this dramatic picture is painted over and over again.

[16] *Review and Herald,* December 15, 1904.

[17] Ellen White, *Review and Herald,* November 22, 1892.

[18] Letter 82, 1888; *Selected Messages,* Book 3, p. 178.

[19] MS 9, 1888.

[20] Revelation 12:17.

[21] Revelation 3:14-21.

[22] Isaiah 63:9.

WHY DO WE LOSE SO MANY
OF OUR YOUTH?

Thoughtful Seventh-day Adventist young people are fundamentally different from youth of Catholic or Protestant denominations who often maintain loyalty to their church because of family ancestry.

Adventist youth seldom have religious roots momentum behind them. They are "present truth" oriented. And they can't be neutral about their religion. If it makes sense, their devotion is all-out. But if it doesn't, they tend to throw devotion to the winds—names on the church books; hearts in the world.

Nominal Catholic or Protestant church membership is respectable. But unless he is sheltered in an Adventist "ghetto," the "traditional" Adventist youth living in today's world can find it hard to cope with the demands of his church's standards. The pressures in a secular world are severe enough, but when other Christians as well disparage Adventist convictions, you ask yourself if being Seventh-day Adventist is worthwhile.

Conservative estimates say we lose vital connection with about half of our youth by the time they reach 18. Some drift off without formally cutting their ties, but many reject the church purposefully and "actually sever their church connections."[1] Of the remainder, not many seem eager to reproduce the zeal of former "missionary volunteers." Almost any alert church board can observe first-hand this hemorrhage of youth loyalty.

Through the decades, thoughtful investigations have noted this urgent problem. An investigation by Charles Martin four decades ago revealed that only about half then agreed that "the doctrines are clear to me and I believe them."[2] Then came a 1971 study that documented even further erosion of religious conviction.[3] By 1973 a similar sampling showed the percentage had dropped to about a third.[4]

In his most recent book, *Why Our Teenagers Leave the Church* (Review and Herald, 2000), Roger A. Dudley reports little if any serious progress: "What percent of our youth are dropping out of the church? ... Most of us sense that the situation is bad."[5]

A knowledgeable educator said in 1978, "A significant stream of Adventist teenagers turn their backs on the values we hold so dear." "Almost every thinking adult is concerned with the slippage among adolescent members. Hand-wringing is common. It is not unusual to hear remarks such as, 'We're spending huge sums for evangelism to bring new converts in the front door of the church while our own young people are streaming out the back door.'"[6] In his 2000 book Dudley quotes an observant young adult, "My church ... invest most of their time and effort in outreach to the community by seminars and door-to-door evangelism—at the same time looking away as the youth slip out the back door of their own church."[7]

The usual pat solution suggested is to send more youth to Adventist educational institutions. But these professional studies largely concern youth who are already in our schools! A more recent one found that "of those who at some time during the 10 years [of this latest survey] dropped out of the church or became inactive, 58 percent took all or most of their education in our schools."[8] Could Ellen White have put her finger on the true source of the problem? She said that there is a heart-gripping, heart-warming truth that "the Lord in His great mercy sent" to Seventh-day Adventists in 1888 which has "in a great degree" been "kept away" from our youth.[9] The few who were exposed to it at that time found it refreshing Good News that warmed their hearts.[10] The same power is still in the message.

A New Development

A four-part series in the *Adventist Review* entitled "To Catch a Star" disclosed that the problem has become denominationally embarrassing. Now we find numbers of Adventist youth joining other churches. "Not exciting, not positive, not big enough, and not related to life"—these are "the specific inadequacies" that they see in today's Adventism. So they are now joining the "Baptists, Presbyterians, Lutherans, Episcopalians, and Catholics," says the *Review* series. These formerly Adventist youth see "denominational distinctiveness ... as of lesser importance than a general belief in a Supreme Being."[11] The more recent proliferation of anti-Adventist propaganda emanating from young ex-Adventist ministers such as Dale Ratzlaff is shaking young Adventists. Ratzlaff hits a raw nerve by saying that Adventist theology is old covenant in nature; the disaffected youth already declaim loudly against what they perceive as love-less legalism predominant in many Adventist churches.[12]

Thank God that some of our youth are happy in their religion and express solid commitment to this church and its unique message. They are precious! But for every one such there are three others the surveys say have lost their way since Primary or Pathfinder days. The *Adventist Review* says flatly: "The church is losing its young people," period.[13]

And even among those who remain, self-sacrificing devotion seems uncommon. Dudley reminds us, "It's one thing to be listed as still being a member of the church. It's quite another to be an active, participating member."[14] Calls for professionally trained personnel to go to difficult mission fields are not easily filled. Those who find paid employment within the church organizations naturally and easily profess Adventism; others may preserve their ties because their social life centers around the church. But a physical presence in the church can often mask a deep spiritual emptiness. In their church fellowship they may not be meeting the Lord Jesus Christ personally.

To reproduce the pioneers' all-consuming devotion "to catch a star" we need some nutriment lacking in our standard spiritual dietary. Jesus says that He is "the Word," and we must "eat" Him. The problem is not that our youth are worse than previous generations; *there is spiritual malnourishment.*

Typical attitudes of many indicate that somewhere between the Cradle Roll and university graduation a fear-motivated distortion of the third angel's message takes over. And fear does not hold them when the world's temptations come barging in. A bird-in-the-hand pleasure is worth two-in-the-new-earth future, and the fear of losing out on the thrills of this world eclipses fear of losing the world to come. Dread of hell and hope of reward in heaven have become bankrupt motivations.

Here are some documented remarks of youth about Adventism.

It would be impossible for them to say these things if they understood the Good News in the New Testament "everlasting gospel" as "the third angel's message in verity."[15]

"Dull, and it gets in the way."

"It's just a bunch of do's and don'ts."

"I don't have any feelings toward it."

"No fun on Saturdays until the sun is down."

"A ritual-type thing. Emotional ups and downs."

The signs of the times indicate how prophecy is being fulfilled, and to them that means a horrible future. They wonder how can they ever endure the time of trouble. It's too difficult to be good. Being a committed Seventh-day Adventist in modern society seems an uphill struggle; few have the guts. Here are more typical remarks, recorded by Roger Dudley:

"I believe in it. I understand it. But I don't know whether I'll be able to stand up for it when the time of trouble comes! I'm afraid of that time!" (Somehow Adventist kids have nightmares about the time of trouble and horrifying dreams of Christ coming when they are not ready.)

"I have a lot of work to do if I want to be saved."

"I wish I could be completely good, but it's not always easy."

"I want to serve God, but I find it very hard."

"I couldn't go through life with all those do's and don'ts. But I guess I have to if I want to go to heaven."[16] In his most recent book Dudley chronicles first-hand reports from many youth who have become alienated from Christ by their Adventist fellowship.

Testimonies of youth are often the realistic, unmasked, tell-it-as-it-is attitudes adults have but they mask their feelings.

Youth Are Not the Only Problem

The overall attrition rate of church membership for both youth and adults in North America, some say, totals more than 50 per cent of new accessions. Many more drop out who are not reported because church boards are loath to update statistics. For every two new members we gain, estimates say we lose about one. What's the problem?

Why is it that the closer we come to the second coming of Christ, the less we are motivated by the Good News about it? Is it because sin has now become "more abounding" than it was in our pioneer era? Or could it be that we don't see that "much more abounding grace" clearly focused?

There seem to be two distortions of Adventism which have filtered down to us through the avenue of our denominational history:

(1) One is the rigid, authoritarian, toe-the-line cult of conformity to rules and external standards. This performance-motif is understood as demanded on pain of a rejection slip in the investigative judgment. Arch-conservatives are good at quoting excerpts from Ellen White selected to produce in youthful minds an impression of sledge-hammer force. Then the youth discover that other churches don't have this severe "Spirit of Prophecy standard" that causes guilt.

The idea has been almost universal that it's virtually impossible to obey God's law so it's hard to be saved and easy to be lost. God has done His part long ago, as the teacher has done his part in dishing out the academy or college course content, and now it's up to us to do our part by shaping up.

For many, this is the traditional Adventist "gospel." They often feel that they can't shape up. Whether or not their impression is fair is not our point; *this is what they have picked up,* and this is what matters.

(2) The opposite extreme is especially in academic communities—a relaxed attitude of *laissez-faire* liberalism. It tends to downplay the necessity or even possibility of true obedience to God's law. He knows we can't keep it properly, and therefore doesn't seriously expect us to. Try to be moral if you can, but if it's not easy, trust His indulgent, grandfatherly softness. He will excuse you. "Occasional lapses" of moral failure are par for the course (that's a popular phrase). Since Jesus is our vicarious Substitute, His perfect obedience must always be a mythical experience impossible for us. The more relaxed atmosphere of non-Adventist churches since 1844 has been right all along, and Adventists have been naive to be so concerned about obedience to God's law. So says this alternative Adventist "gospel." There is wrong on both sides and there is good on both sides, two extremes of a thesis and antithesis, each a protesting reaction against the other. They produce confusion among youth. The traditional arch-conservative philosophy generates resentment, alienation, and rebellion; or if one imagines he measures up, pride.

Youth Caught in a No Man's Land

Ellen White statements (out of context, of course) can be compiled in such a way as to portray God as a stern teacher who dishes out his lecture content and leaves us to sink or swim when exam time comes. Youth picture Him as pointing out the steep path to salvation: "You want to go to heaven? It's a rough, rocky, thorny way; I hope you make it. Many don't. I won't be surprised if you don't. I have someone else waiting to take your crown." Many feel that their absence from heaven wouldn't be missed. Why bother? Why lose *both* worlds?

The opposite is an Adventist species of antinomianism which arrogantly flaunts worldliness and sensuality in the face of divine warnings. But as surely as rigid traditionalism *drives* people out of the church, so this "new theology" *entices* them out.

The story of 1888 brings refreshing Good News, reminding us that since "the curse causeless shall not come"[17] *it has never been God's will that we lose our youth.* The cause is real and the problem can be corrected. "With such an army as our youth" when they are informed and challenged by "the third angel's message in verity," the world can indeed be lightened with the glory of the gospel.

The Long Delay Has Not Been God's Will

A general malaise of denominational lukewarmness is not inherent in our doctrines or in our denominational identity. *It is "in a great degree" the consequence of losing the 1888 message.* It's refreshing to note that something positive can be done about it.

There has been a vacuum into which have rushed these alternative heresies of rigid traditionalism and loose antinomianism. Both deny essentials of the 1888 message, yet both are starved for its unique nutritive elements. Neither could flourish within the church, surely not bear fruit, were it not for the "in-a-great-measure" famine for that "most precious message."[18] Adventist youth could not label Adventism "not exciting, not positive, not big enough, and not related to life" if they understood the 1888 message. Is Christ "not exciting, ... not big enough, and not related to life"? As the true Leader of this church He is intensely interesting! It's not the fault of youth that the vision that shone so brightly in the 1888 message has been "in a great degree" denied them.[19]

The 1888 message was supremely "exciting," "positive," "big," and "related to life." It kindled a "first love" experience in the hearts of those who heard it. There are definite reasons why:

(1) It cut the Gordian knot of self-centered motivation. It restored the pure New Testament motivation of a heart-appreciation of the love of Christ. Through the utter simplicity of the message of the cross it abolished both the fear that discourages youth today and the boredom that wearies them.

(2) It revealed Christ as One whose love is active, not passive. He was seen as a Good Shepherd looking for His lost sheep rather than vice versa. It made clear that salvation does not depend on our holding on to God's hand but on our believing that He is holding on to our hand. In a practical way which transcended theological hairsplitting, the gospel became a message of salvation by grace through faith alone—faith *which works,* not faith *and works.*

(3) Christ was presented as a Savior "nigh at hand," not "afar off," refreshingly different from ideas held in common by the Evangelicals of the day. The popular idea that Christ took only the unfallen, sinless nature of Adam in Eden was exposed as a legacy of Roman Catholicism. The idea far transcended a theological dispute: it was beautiful "practical godliness."

(4) Justification by faith was lifted above doctrinal hair-splitting to be a vital message of union with Christ. The devotion to Christ displayed by the apostles becomes not only possible but certain, *if this message is understood.*

(5) The two covenants, a "doctrine" often regarded as a dry-as-dust theological bore, became one that gripped hearts. Jones' and Waggoner's idea began to penetrate dark corners of Adventist understanding.[20]

(6) The unique truth that was the foundation of Seventh-day Adventist existence came alive in the 1888 message like resurrected dry bones in Ezekiel's vision—the cleansing of the heavenly sanctuary. Again, "doctrine" transcended theology and became practical godliness.

An 1889 hymn expresses something of its thrill:

"I sing the love of Christ, my Saviour,
Who suffered upon the tree,
That in the secret of His presence,
My bondage might freedom be.
He comes to 'bind the broken hearted;'
He comes the fainting soul to cheer;
He gives me 'oil of joy for mourning,' and 'beauty for ashes' here.

"I sing the beauty of the Gospel
That scatters not thorns, but flow'rs,
That bids me scatter smiles and sunbeams
Wherever are lonely hours.
The 'garment of His praise' it offers
For 'heaviness of spirit,' drear;
It gives me sunshine for my shadow,
And 'beauty for ashes' here."

—J. G. Crabbe

Youth of a century ago who had the privilege of hearing the message were captivated by it.[21] Youth of today who get a chance to hear it sense the same phenomena. The enticements of sensuality, appetite, wealth, leisure and pleasure, the upwardly mobile instinct, the allurements of our scintillating electronic age, all lose their charm for the one who has seen and appreciates that message of Christ's righteousness.

Chapter Two Endnotes

[1] See Roger L. Dudley, *Why Teenagers Reject Religion,* (Review and Herald, 1978), pp. 20, 21, and his up-dated 2000, *Why Our Teenagers Leave the Church,* statistic on the back cover.

[2] Charles D. Martin, "Moral and Religious Problems and Attitudes as Expressed by Students in Four Seventh-day Adventist Academies," M. A. Thesis, Andrews University.

[3] Joel N. Noble, "Certain Religious and Educational Attitudes of Senior High School Students in Seventh-day Adventist Schools in the Pacific Northwest," Ph. D. dissertation, University of Oregon, 1971.

[4] Stanley G. Hardt, M. A. thesis, Andrews University, 1973.

[5] *Why Our Teenagers Leave the Church,* p. 27.

[6] Roger L. Dudley, op. cit., pp. 11, 13.

[7] *Why Our Teenagers Leave the Church,* p. 166.

[8] Ibid., p. 160.

[9] *Selected Messages,* Book One, pp. 234, 235.

[10] Ellen G. White, *Review and Herald,* March 5, 1889.

[11] *Adventist Review,* June, 1986.

[12] See Dudley, *Why Our Teenagers Leave the Church,* chapter 6.

[13] June 2, 1988.

[14] *Op. cit.,* p. 35.

[15] Cf. Ellen G. White, *Review and Herald,* April 1, 1890.

[16] Dudley, *Why Teenagers Reject Religion,* pp. 9, 17.

[17] Proverbs 26:2.

[18] Cf. *Selected Messages,* Book One, pp. 234, 235; *Testimonies to Ministers,* p. 91.

[19] *Ibid.*

[20] In 1907 significant steps were taken by the Review and Herald and Pacific Press publishers to abandon the 1888 message view of God's covenant as His one-sided promise, and to substitute the anti-1888 view that His covenant was a contract.

[21] Cf. Ellen G. White, *Review and Herald,* March 5, 1889, concerning meetings at the school in South Lancaster when Jones and Waggoner spoke.

Chapter Three

CHRIST'S COMING: HOW SOON IS "SOON"?

The dictionary defines an "Adventist" as a person who believes that Christ's second coming is *near*. More than that, the name means one who *loves the thought* that it is near.

The Seventh-day Adventist Church sprang from a phenomenal conviction in the hearts of some humble Christians who discovered in the Bible a prophetic road map. To them Daniel and Revelation revealed that mankind's weary journey in this world of sin was about at its end. To them this was great Good News. Our Adventist roots go back to when many Christians of different denominations first saw these prophetic books as "unsealed."

Thus Adventism burst upon the Christian world as almost a new revelation. A few individuals through the centuries had spoken of the second coming as near, but no significant movement had ever risen which clearly understood how a connected series of Bible prophecies *proved* that His return was near. It was as though the church had been sleeping like Rip Van Winkle for nearly eighteen hundred years and suddenly awoke to a new experience—anticipating this glorious event. This phenomenal new life followed the end of the prophetic period of 1260 years when Daniel's "time of the end" began in 1798.[1]

Thousands rejoiced to trace these "waymarks" on the prophetic roadmap. The personal return of the beloved Savior in their lifetime became a "blessed hope." The thought of His return and setting up His kingdom was equivalent to what winning the sweepstakes would be to us.

And this was not because they longed for relief from 18th century physical toil and privation; their hearts were in union with Christ. Because they sensed some appreciation for His character of love, they wanted Him to return. For that group of Christians of many different churches, there was no self-centered motivation to cloud the bright flame of their devotion to Christ.

A "First" Since Apostolic Times

The 1840s movement was thus the first time since the apostles where Jesus could find a community of believers on earth whose hearts were knit with His in joyful expectation of His soon return. They were among those of whom Jesus said, "Blessed are they that have not seen, and yet have believed."[2]

This is why devotion similar to that of Pentecost marked them. It leaped across the centuries like fire blown by the wind. Joseph Bates spent his life savings spreading the message so that he came to face old age nearly penniless. Uriah Smith gave up a promising career for the toil and privations of Adventist editing. His sister Annie prematurely burned out the strength of her youth. Others sold farms and gave the proceeds to the cause. Young people such as the Loughboroughs and James and Ellen White threw themselves wholeheartedly into sacrificial living. The taste of this kind of Adventism was in their "mouth sweet as honey."[3]

The yellowed pages of their letters and journals testify to the joy they cherished. They actually loved the thought of the coming of Christ! A bride's anticipation of union with her bridegroom depicts the thrill of the message that gave birth to the Seventh-day Adventist Church. Cold theology and prosaic mathematics unraveling Daniel's 2300 or 1290 days could never stir human hearts and emotions like that. The church was about to welcome a Loved One absent a long, long time. It was not superficial emotionalism, but a gripping experience that Ellen White called "heartwork."[4] There was pure, authentic joy of heart, the all-risking abandon that some youth seek vainly in a drug-induced "high" but never attain, because they find only its counterfeit.

All infatuation of illicit love, all idolatry even of valid human love, is a vain search for a reality that exists only in the true Christ. The mysterious charm that shines in an attractive human face is only a dim reflection of the light of His face. Romeo and Juliet die for a failure to see Him. Gilda sings her beautiful "Caro Nome" in *Rigoletto* to express her love for her Walter, not knowing that the only name that thrills forever is that of Jesus.

The youth who pioneered the Seventh-day Adventist Church needed no chemical dependency, no alcohol, no *affaire de coeur,* to relieve soul-boredom. They knew firsthand the thrill that inspired Charles Wesley to sing, "Jesus, Lover of My Soul." They had rediscovered what the youthful Saul of Tarsus found on his way to Damascus when a glorious light blinded his eyes and illumined his soul forever after. Paul was never disobedient to the heavenly vision even up to that day when he glimpsed sunlight for the last time as the headsman's axe fell, and he bequeathed his joy "unto all them also that love His appearing."[5]

This Love Affair with Christ is True Adventism

The all-too-common motivation of fear of judgment and hope of personal reward in heaven is a pathetic distortion of Adventism. Our youthful pioneers tapped into the phenomenal faith that gripped the hearts of apostolic Christians. For these early Adventists, to be with Jesus was heaven enough because their hearts appreciated the love that led Him to His cross. Sabbath-keeping in difficult economic conditions was not too much sacrifice to make for truth. No missionary service, no exile of ministry in lonely "dark" foreign land, was too arduous a deprivation. Calls to service elicited no questions about the pay, the perks, the climate, or terms of service. Medical or retirement "benefits" never crossed their minds. Jesus said "Go ye!" and *fellowship with Him* was remuneration enough. Their faith was expressed by one of them:

> May 14, 1851, I saw the beauty and loveliness of Jesus. As I beheld His glory, the thought did not occur to me that I should ever be separated from His presence.[6]

The thought of "the blessed hope" sustained them through trials that we find more difficult to endure as its nearness recedes from our modern vision.

For example, as early as 1850 Ellen White was saying:

> Some are looking too far off for the coming of the Lord. Time has continued a few years longer than they expected. ... I saw that

the time for Jesus to be in the most holy place was nearly finished, and that time can last but a very little longer.[7]

One of her last appeals is unusually fervent:

The coming of Christ is near, and hasteth greatly. The time in which to labor is short, and men and women are perishing. Said the angel, "Should not the men who have had great light co-operate with Him who sent His Son to the world to give light and salvation to men?"[8]

How Soon Is "Soon"?

Can we continue forever saying that the return of Christ is "soon"? Why has time continued for so many decades after the Lord's servant said that it "is near," and "time … is short"?

She said something at a conference of believers in Battle Creek in May, 1856 that has now become perplexing and even embarrassing to explain:

I was shown the company present at the Conference. Said the angel, "Some food for worms, some subjects of the seven last plagues, some will be alive and remain upon the earth to be translated at the coming of Jesus."[9]

This is a stumbling block to some because of the obvious fact that *all* who were "present at the Conference" in 1856 have become "food for worms," and *none* are "alive and remain." Was Ellen White a false prophet?

In seeking to defend her credibility it is common to say that such a prophecy is "conditional," that is, its fulfillment depends on the faithfulness of God's people. But this explanation can also widen still further the gap of Ellen White's credibility. If the prophecies that declare the end to be near are "conditional" on the faithfulness of God's people, what will happen if God's people forever prove to be unfaithful? This explanation can imply terribly bad news. So far, because of our unbelief, time has continued far beyond what it should have. Will the end therefore never be truly near? How soon is "near"?

Ellen White's credibility is not at issue. She was merely reporting what she heard *the "angel"* say. She herself never offered her own personal prediction that people alive in 1856 would see the Lord come without tasting death. *"The angel" said so.*

Someone may object that this makes matters worse: now it appears that we can't trust the angels. No. The angel was sincere and in his perfect right to make this statement in 1856 when the Laodicean message was first understood and accepted by God's remnant people. It was the influence of holy angels who brought to the hearts of early Adventists the conviction that the loud cry would begin within the lifetime of people at the conference in 1856. And Jesus tells us that no "angels which are in heaven" know the actual time of His second coming.[10]

But even though he is not omniscient, the angel used good angelic common sense. From his knowledge of the holy prophecies and of the repentant faith of the early believers in 1856, he had every reason to expect that in those "days of the voice of the seventh angel, when he shall begin to sound, the mystery of God should be finished, as he hath declared to his servants the prophets."[11] The angel knew that the final cosmic Day of Atonement had begun at the end of the 2300 "days" (years), when the heavenly sanctuary should at last be cleansed. Something was to happen that had never happened in previous history. The angel was happy that a "little flock" were accepting every ray of light that came from heaven, step by step. Here were a people on earth whose hearts were in sympathy with Christ's closing work as our great High Priest. Now the end *can* come "soon"!

Heaven Did Not Let the Angel Down

In precise fulfillment of the 1856 vision, the Lord sent the "beginning" of the latter rain and of the loud cry 32 years later, well within the lifetime of people at the 1856 Battle Creek conference. A marvelous event occurred at that humble gathering of Adventist leaders in the Minneapolis Seventh-day Adventist Church:

> The time of test is just upon us, for the loud cry of the third angel has already begun *in the revelation of the righteousness of Christ,*

the sin-pardoning Redeemer. This is the beginning of the light of the angel whose glory shall fill the whole earth.[12]

This had never happened before. Thoughtful church members were thrilled by a statement by G. B. Starr sent from Australia at the 1893 General Conference Session: "Sister White says that we have been in the time of the latter rain since the Minneapolis meeting."[13]

Although she said several times that the end could have come at various times between 1844 and 1888 if God's people had been faithful, she never said that it could have come without the latter rain falling first. No grain can get ripe for a harvest without it. Therefore any statements that say the end could have come before 1888 must be understood as requiring that the latter rain and the loud cry message would have to come first. But never at any time did Ellen White declare that such had begun in any message or revival *prior to 1888.*

There is a difference between the early rain outpouring of the Holy Spirit and that of the latter rain. Jesus likens His church to a garden crop to be harvested:

"The kingdom of God is as if a man should scatter seed on the ground, and should sleep by night and rise by day, and the seed should sprout and grow, he himself does not know how. For the earth yields crops by itself: first the blade, then the head, after that the full grain in the head. But when the grain ripens, immediately he puts in the sickle, because the harvest has come."[14]

Does "the harvest" come when people die, or at the second coming of Christ? There is an answer in Revelation:

And I looked, and behold, a white cloud, and on the cloud sat One like the Son of Man, having on His head a golden crown, and in His hand a sharp sickle. And another angel came out of the temple, crying with a loud voice to Him who sat on the cloud, "Thrust in Your sickle and reap, for the harvest of the earth is ripe." So He who sat on the cloud thrust in His sickle on the earth, and the earth was reaped.[15]

The One who went to the cross for the world, who poured out His soul unto death, who suffered unspeakable agonies for our redemption, looks upon that ripened "grain" as the hard-won, precious fruit of His sacrifice. He deserves it.

All of earth's thousands of years of history have been the growing season preparatory to this moment of "harvest" when He personally returns. Out of earth's billions of all ages now comes at last a corporate remnant of precious souls who gladly receive the showers of the latter rain. Their mature faith as a community of believers has at last reflected the beauty of Christ's character. Without fail, "the great, grand work of bringing out a people who will have Christlike characters, and who will be able to stand in the day of the Lord, is to be accomplished."[16]

This is what the angel in 1856 was hoping for. It is the "practical godliness" fruitage of the cleansing of the sanctuary. "Just as soon as the people of God are sealed in their foreheads—it is not any seal or mark that can be seen, but a settling into the truth, both intellectually and spiritually, so they cannot be moved—just as soon as God's people are sealed and prepared for the shaking, it will come."[17] Tons of ore have at last yielded an ounce of purest gold. Heaven rejoices that the sacrifice of Christ is fully rewarded in a people whose mature faith has produced mature righteousness. At last, righteousness by faith has come into its own. No wonder the angel was happy in 1856:

> Christ is waiting with longing desire for the manifestation of Himself in His church. When the character of Christ shall be perfectly reproduced in His people, then He will come to claim them as His own.[18]

It's Not a Do-It-Yourself Works Program

Note that no one prepares himself or herself for "the harvest." *The latter rain causes the grain to ripen.* Our part is to *welcome* that blessing, and not to fight it off in the weirdest resistance time has ever known. Grown-up faith *works,* producing perfect righteousness.

Ever since early days, Seventh-day Adventists have looked forward to the latter rain. As she saw it in vision Ellen White's description quickens the pulse:

I heard those clothed with the armor speak forth the truth with great power. It had effect. Many had been bound; some wives by their husbands, and some children by their parents. The honest who had been prevented from hearing the truth now eagerly laid hold upon it. All fear of their relatives was gone, and the truth alone was exalted to them. … It was dearer and more precious than life. I asked what had made this great change. An angel answered, "It is the latter rain, the refreshing from the presence of the Lord, the loud cry of the third angel."[19]

The *early rain* fell at Pentecost, and has been received ever since through the past two thousand years as untold multitudes of human souls have prepared for death.

But there must come a change before Christ's second coming. A people must now be prepared, not for death, but for translation without seeing death. Another great outpouring of the Holy Spirit will accomplish a work that "makes ready a people," a church, a community, of believers. It also empowers them to complete the great unfinished commission of proclaiming the everlasting gospel to all the world. This final outpouring of the Holy Spirit is the *latter rain*.

It's Weird: Praying for Something While It's Resisted

The truth of our history indicates that all the while we have been praying for the gift to come during this past century and more, there is evidence that we have unwittingly been resisting it. Our brethren who prayed for it between 1856 and 1888 resisted it when it finally came, just as the Jews who prayed for the coming of their Messiah for two thousand years rejected Him when He came. Maybe we are repeating the syndrome. What could be more foolish than resisting something you're praying for?

Some feel discouraged because they think that this syndrome of rejecting heaven's blessing must continue on and on. But this is not, cannot be, true. Grace must not forever be on trial.

Because the kingdoms of Israel and Judah were unfaithful in ancient times, and because the Jews rejected Christ, and because the Christian church has done little better, some mournfully conclude that the organized remnant church today has as well doomed itself to ultimate failure.

But there is a truth that these sincere ones have overlooked. The Lord has staked His eternal honor on His word: "Unto two thousand three hundred days [years ending in 1844] then shall the sanctuary be cleansed."[20]

This Bible truth is "most precious" Good News. It is unique to Seventh-day Adventists, the foundation of their denominational existence. Something is to happen in this cosmic Day of Atonement that has never happened before. And here we come to the mysterious parting of the ways between faith and unbelief. *Faith believes that prophecy of Daniel and cooperates with the great High Priest in His closing work of atonement.*

Such faith will cease resisting the latter rain blessing. It will surrender to the cross whereon self is crucified "with Christ." God has chosen to exercise faith in His people that they will not let Him down,[21] and the previously unending syndrome of unbelief and unfaithfulness is at last broken.

Getting ready *while still alive* to meet the Judge of all the earth face to face when He returns personally the second time—this strikes terror to many stout hearts. Those who blithely dismiss this experience as nothing serious just haven't given thought to it. But the 1888 message was sent to assuage this fear and to prepare a people for the end.

From Pentecost to 1888 many honest, sincere hearts rejoiced to receive the gift of the Holy Spirit, but it was always the *early rain*. During that time, there was no latter rain. A distinct line of demarcation exists between the early rain and the latter rain, and 1888 is that dividing line.

These facts help us tremendously to understand the mystery of the long delay in the return of Christ. Our early pioneers' faith in His soon coming was not rustic naiveté. Sober Holy Scripture did indeed support their convictions. The early apostles would have welcomed the latter rain if they had been alive in 1888. The delay is not God's fault. True faith in Christ's closing work of atonement will resolve the confusion and make "soon" become soon.

What Adventism Should Have Been

The world stage in the nineteenth century was set for the end of the reign of sin and suffering. Events in the political world, the juxtaposition of Islam, Catholicism, Protestantism, and paganism, were a perfect lineup of the scenario of Daniel and Revelation. It is astounding but true that before the inventions of radio, TV, jet travel, satellites, the web and computers, it would have been quicker to take the message to the whole world of that day than is our task today.

The proclamation of the gospel of Christ requires effective communication of one human heart to another, not merely visual or audio exposure to electronic stimuli. The avenues of that effective communication were open in the 1888 era; it was easier to grip the attention of people then than it is now. Our most effective electronic presentations today are quickly drowned out by the never-ending flood of sophisticated entertainment often inspired by Satan.

By neglecting our 1888 opportunity we have made our task more difficult today, so much so that for many Seventh-day Adventists, especially youth, the entire prophetic picture has slipped out of focus. So vast and complex are the needs for social betterment of world population that many now can see only unending years of "social gospel" work. For example, millions caught in chemical and alcohol dependency and poor diet need physical deliverance before they can even begin to comprehend the gospel. Hundreds of millions, even billions, are so ground down by the economic struggle to survive in crowded urban and village existence that they can hardly "hear" our message. And further millions exist under the shadow of AIDS.

A Century of Delay Intensifies Our Problem

A major segment of the world is held in such an iron-fisted grip that for many Seventh-day Adventists the third angel's warning against "the mark of the beast" now appears archaic and irrelevant. The weary passage of more than a century of mysterious delay has antiquated Adventism in their thinking.

To many of this generation the Papacy no longer appears to be the "beast." Now, they think, it must be some other world power. Prophetic certainties we held in the past raise questions. Both "liberals" and "conservatives" try to reinterpret Daniel and Revelation, few if any agreeing with each other, and all succeeding only in deepening the confusion by what Ellen White called "new theories."

Can we get the prophetic picture back into focus again?

Yes, but not by trying to reinterpret the prophecies. The first step is to recover what we lost in 1888. There we will find solid truth confirmed by the gift of the Spirit of Prophecy. Once that picture comes into focus, a unified conviction will once again make sense of the prophecies.

Fortunately, the "beginning" of the latter rain and the loud cry was not just an emotional, elusive revival in the church. It was objective truth in the *message* of Christ's righteousness. That is something that we *can* recover.

Our youth will listen, and be moved.

Chapter Three Endnotes

[1] Daniel 7:25; 11:33-35; 12:4; Revelation 12:6,14; 13:5.

[2] John 20:29.

[3] See Revelation 10:9.

[4] See *Testimonies for the Church,* Vol. 1, p. 663; Vol. 4, p. 601; Vol. 5, p. 306.

[5] 2 Timothy 4:8.

[6] *Early Writings,* p. 70.

[7] *Ibid.,* p. 58.

[8] *Testimonies for the Church,* Vol. 9, p. 105; 1909.

[9] *Ibid.,* Vol. 1, pp. 131, 132.

[10] Mark 13:32.

[11] Revelation 10:7.

[12] *Review and Herald,* November 22, 1892; *Selected Messages,* Book One, p. 363; A. G. Daniells, *Christ Our Righteousness,* p. 56; see also *Selected Messages,* Book One, pp. 234, 235.

[13] *General Conference Bulletin,* 1893, p. 377.

[14] Mark 4:26-29, NKJV.

[15] Revelation 14:14-16, NKJV.

[16] *Testimonies for the Church,* Vol. 6, p. 129.

[17] *Seventh-day Adventist Bible Commentary,* Vol. 4, p. 1161.

[18] *Christ's Object Lessons,* p. 69.

[19] *Early Writings,* p. 271.

[20] Daniel 8:14.

[21] See Galatians 2:20; Romans 3:3, 4.

IF IT ISN'T INTERESTING, MAYBE IT ISN'T TRUE

The word "gospel" means "Good News," and Heaven forbid, it's never boring. Correctly presented, it always captures and holds people's attention. When Jesus proclaimed the News, "the common people heard him gladly."[1] The apostles' preaching was so attractive and winning that their enemies confessed that they had "turned the world upside down."[2] In every age, the Good News compels the attention of mankind. Never does the Holy Spirit indite a tame, stale message. The last proclamation is communicated by "angels" "to those who dwell on the earth—to every nation, tribe, tongue, and people, … *with a loud voice,*" meaning, with compelling interest. Then the message swells "mightily" as it lightens the earth with glory.[3] Turns towns and cities "upside down."

This scenario must call for the most interesting and powerful communication that the world has ever heard. Yawning and neutrality will become impossible. As in the days of the apostles, people will get off the fence and either accept wholeheartedly or reject just as decidedly. For everyone it's going to be one or the other, either the final mark of the beast or the seal of God.

Any presentation of the gospel that is dull is suspect. The Adventist youth who complain of Adventism as "not exciting, not positive, not big enough" most likely have never heard that third angel's message proclaimed "in verity" in the way that catalyzes humanity.

The 1888 message lifted Adventist preaching and teaching out of the doldrums. Ellen White describes its impact on youth:

> Meetings were held in the College which were intensely interesting. … The Christian life, which had before seemed to them [the students] undesirable and full of inconsistencies, now

41

appeared in its true light, in remarkable symmetry and beauty. He who had been to them as a root out of dry ground, without form or comeliness, became "the chiefest among ten thousand," and the one "altogether lovely." ... One after another of these students of Battle Creek College, hitherto ignorant of the truth and of the saving grace of God, espoused the cause of Christ....

[Listeners] expressed ... gladness and gratitude of heart for the sermons that had been preached by Bro. A. T. Jones; they saw the truth, goodness, mercy, and love of God as they never before had seen it.[4]

Two of Ellen White's favorite words to describe the 1888 message were "precious" and "most precious."[5] Her vocabulary of enthusiastic endorsement of the message and ministry of Jones and Waggoner nearly exhausts the English language treasury of enthusiasm. The following is an assortment of these phrases culled verbatim from her writings between 1888 and 1896:

"God has given them His message;" "presented with freshness and power;" "Christ's delegated messengers;" "men whom God has commissioned;""the demonstration of the Holy Spirit;""men divinely appointed;" [there is] "beauty in the precious things presented at this [1888] Conference ... convincing evidence;" "most precious light;" "precious truths;" "the waves of truth;" "harmonizes perfectly with the light which God has been pleased to give me during all the years of my experience;""this message ... will lighten the earth with its glory;" "it was the first clear [public] teaching about this subject from any human lips I have heard;""in Minneapolis God gave precious gems of truth to His people in new settings;""this light ... [is] the matchless charms of Christ;""God sent these young men [Jones and Waggoner] to bear a special message;""God has committed to His servants a message for this time;""His chosen servants;""the true religion, the only religion of the Bible ... that advocates righteousness by the faith of the Son of God;" "showers of the latter rain from heaven ... in Minneapolis;""men upon whom God has laid the burden of a solemn work;" "God is working through these instrumentalities;" "through brethren Jones and Waggoner; ... these men had a message from God;" "God has upheld them; ... He has given them precious light, and their message has fed the people of God;" "in rejecting the message given at Minneapolis, men committed sin;" "light from the throne of God;" "the message of His healing grace;" "if you accept the message, you accept Jesus;" "every fiber of my heart said Amen;" "the manifest movement of the Spirit of God;" "Brother Jones has borne the message ... and light and freedom and the outpouring of the Spirit of God has attended the work. ... 'Messengers I [the Lord] sent to My people with light, with grace and power;'" "great and glorious truths;" "a Christ-like spirit manifested, such as Elder E.J. Waggoner had shown ... like a Christian gentleman ... in a kind and courteous manner;" "the voice of the true Shepherd;" "wherever this message comes, its fruits are good ... great treasures of truth. ... A life-giving message ... to give life to the dry bones," "the deep movings of the Spirit of God have been felt upon almost every heart. ... We seemed to breathe in the very atmosphere of Heaven;" "the present message ... bears the divine credentials;" "the Lord is giving fresh evidence of His truth, placing it in a new setting, that the way of the Lord may be prepared;" "we have been hearing [Christ's] voice in the message that has been going for the last two years [1890];" "the message He has sent us during these last two years is from Heaven;" "the heavenly credentials;" "it is the third angel's message in verity;" "messages bearing the divine credentials ... set forth among us with beauty and loveliness, to charm all whose hearts are not closed with prejudice;" "new wine ... additional light;" "Brother Jones speaks ... [the people] fed with large morsels from the Lord's table;" "heaven-sent refreshing of the shower of grace;" "the voice of the heavenly Merchantman."[6]

This is only a brief sampling of some 375 such expressions. An eye-witness, J.S.Washburn, told us how he remembered seeing Ellen White sit on the front seat at Minneapolis while Waggoner was speaking, her face beaming as she kept saying "Amen! Brethren, there is great light here."[7] She herself confirms this when she says of Waggoner's message, "When [he] presented it, every fiber of my heart said Amen."[8]

Yet most of our people have acquired the idea that there is something dangerous about that message, that in many areas Ellen White disagreed with it. She couldn't have said all those things if she had disagreed with it. In fact, *there is not one area* of the message that she disagreed with when she came to understand it.[9]

Six years later she was still enthusiastically describing the ongoing message as "the sweetest melodies that come from human lips,— justification by faith, and the righteousness of Christ."[10] Imagine a message presented to Seventh-day Adventists so joyous and hope inspiring that the listeners were tempted to think it was too good to be true.[11]

The message is not so much the miracle of feeding hungry people as the greater miracle of developing an appetite in church members so undernourished that they do not even feel hungry. Surely our heavenly Father wants us to learn to appreciate what a blessing a healthy appetite is.

Not only is the Lord our Shepherd, He is also our Host who seats us at His table loaded with nutritious spiritual food. But most of us are not spiritually hungry and thirsty, and many are famished for spiritual food. Day after day, week after week passes, without personally ingesting the bread of life. A millionaire starving with no appetite may be worse off than a famine refugee who feels his hunger.

If the Lord's messenger were among us today, she would have to say again, "This I do know, that our churches are dying for the want of teaching on the subject of righteousness by faith in Christ, and on kindred truths."[12]

The Inestimable Blessing of Feeling Hungry and Thirsty

There is a special happiness that comes when we sense this starvation. "Blessed are those who hunger and thirst for righteousness, for they shall be filled."[13] Here is Ellen White's description of the happiness we will know when we learn to feel that hunger (many said things like this when they heard the 1888 message):

If you have a sense of need in your soul, if you hunger and thirst after righteousness, this is an evidence that Christ has wrought upon your heart. ... Familiar truths will present themselves to your mind in a new aspect; texts of Scripture will burst upon you with a new meaning, as a flash of light. ... You will know that Christ is leading you; a divine Teacher is at your side. ... You ... will long to speak to others of the comforting things that have been revealed to you. ... You will communicate some fresh thought in regard to the character or the work of Christ. You will have some fresh revelation of His pitying love to impart to those who love Him and to those who love Him not.[14]

When the Lord says that we are "blessed" when we hunger after righteousness, what kind of righteousness must He be speaking of? There is only one kind—that which is by faith.

In other words, those who feel that they already understand righteousness by faith lose the blessing straight off, while those who *feel* empty are the only ones who *can* "be filled." There is tragic reality here, for there could even be some ministers and leaders who don't sense their need. Jesus says He actually hears them say in their hearts that they're not hungry.

According to the Lord Jesus, we, both leaders and people, have a basic general problem. He says: "You say, 'I am rich, have become wealthy, and have need of nothing.'"[15] Or, "You don't feel hungry or thirsty." He is describing a last-days phenomenon. As a people generally we feel wealthy in our understanding of the gospel. "We have the truth; we understand the doctrine of righteousness by faith." This feeling of satisfaction dooms us to world embarrassment, for in fact he says we are "wretched, and miserable, and poor," and (in the Greek) outstandingly so.

And, unbelievable as it may seem, the Lord Himself says that the ones who primarily exhibit this lack of healthy appetite are the leadership of His church.[16] The "angel of the church" is not the same as the church. The churches are "the seven golden candlesticks," but "the angel of the church of the Laodiceans" is its leadership, including administrators, educators, pastors, elders, deacons, Sabbath School teachers, Pathfinder leaders, etc. One couldn't dare to say this unless the Lord Himself said it. As a group, He says we share that common illness of feeling full when in fact we are starving.

A Message of Healing for the Seventh-day Adventist Church

There was also spiritual famine among us prior to 1888. A few months before the Minneapolis conference the Lord's messenger declared:

> A revival of true godliness among us is the greatest and most urgent of all our needs. ... We have far more to fear from within than from without. The hindrances to strength and success are far greater from the church itself than from the world. ... What is our condition in this fearful and solemn time? Alas, what pride is prevailing in the church, what hypocrisy, what deception, what love of dress, frivolity, and amusement, what desire for supremacy! All these sins have clouded the mind, so that eternal things have not been discerned.[17]

> The facts concerning the real condition of the professed people of God, speak more loudly than their profession, and make it evident that some power has cut the cable that anchored them to the Eternal Rock, and that they are drifting away to sea, without chart or compass.[18]

The issue that faces us is whether words like the following could apply to us in this new millennium. It's too natural for us to feel that they are passé. A few weeks before the 1888 Conference began, she wrote: "O that the haughty hearts of men ... might enter into the meaning of redemption, and seek to learn the meekness and lowliness of Jesus."[19]

It was this need that the Lord wanted to meet in the message of 1888. These words have been often quoted:

> The Lord in His great mercy sent a most precious message to His people through Elders Waggoner and Jones. This message was to bring more prominently before the world the uplifted Saviour, the sacrifice for the sins of the whole world. It presented justification through faith in the Surety; it invited the people to receive the righteousness of Christ, which is made manifest in obedience to all the commandments of God.[20]

Even though the message was "in a great measure" resisted and kept from the people a century ago, there are beautiful pictures of success that describe the future of God's work. Hope revels in these promises: "This gospel ... will be preached in all the world," said Jesus. "The earth will be filled with the knowledge of the glory of the Lord, as the waters cover the sea." "I will pour out My Spirit on all flesh. ... It shall come to pass that whoever calls on the name of the Lord shall be saved. For in Mount Zion and in Jerusalem there shall be deliverance."[21]

This last message is to be simple, beautiful, and always interesting. The future has to be good:

> If through the grace of Christ His people will become new bottles, He will fill them with the new wine. God will give additional light, and old truths will be recovered, and replaced in the framework of truth. ... One interest will prevail, one subject will swallow up every other,—CHRIST OUR RIGHTEOUSNESS.[22]

As we discover what that "most precious" message is and how it differs from what is commonly assumed to be "the [Evangelical] doctrine of righteousness by faith," we shall find it refreshingly different. The revelation of "the righteousness of Christ" reveals Him as a Savior "nigh at hand" and "not afar off."

It might become Good News far better than most imagine is possible.

Chapter Four Endnotes

[1] Mark 12:37.

[2] Acts 17:6.

[3] Revelation 14:6; 18:1-4.

[4] *Review and Herald,* February 12, 1889.

[5] See *Testimonies to Ministers,* p. 91; Ms. 8a, 1888; Ms. 15, 1888; Ms. 24, 1888; Ms. 13, 1889; *Review and Herald,* March 5, July 23, September 3, 1889; March 11, 1890; August 8, 1893; Letter 51a, 1895.

[6] See Appendix for the list of these sources.

[7] Signed report of interview with J. S. Washburn, Hagerstown, Maryland, June 4, 1950.

[8] Ms. 5, 1889.

[9] There were times when she cautioned the messengers not to overstate their convictions and thus create for themselves unnecessary prejudice. These counsels are sometimes interpreted as disagreements, which is not true. She supported their message heart and soul, as these quoted phrases indicate. The "Majority" Report of the General Conference *ad hoc* "Primacy of the Gospel Committee" (February 8, 2000; www.adventist.org) maintains that there were "many areas" in which Ellen White disagreed with the "most precious message" which "the Lord in His great mercy sent to His people through Elders Waggoner and Jones." This raises a question: how could an honest woman write hundreds of endorsemens of their message and then disagree with even one "area" and not tell us what it was? No evidence exists to support that charge of "many areas."

[10] *Review and Herald,* April 4, 1895.

[11] *Ibid.,* July 23, 1889.

[12] *Gospel Workers,* p. 301.

[13] Matthew 5:6.

[14] *Thoughts From the Mount of Blessing,* p. 36.

[15] Revelation 3:16, 17.

[16] Verse 14; Revelation 1:20; *Gospel Workers,* pp. 13, 14; *Acts of the Apostles,* p. 586.

[17] *Review and Herald,* March 22, 1887.

[18] *Ibid.,* July 24, 1888.

[19] *Ibid.,* September 11, 1888.

[20] *Testimonies to Ministers,* pp. 91, 92.

[21] Matthew 24:14; Revelation 18:1-4; Habakkuk 2:14; Joel 2:28-32.

[22] *Review and Herald,* Extra, December 23, 1890; see Jeremiah 23:6; 33:16; Isaiah 32:17.

Chapter Five

IF IT ISN'T GOOD NEWS, CAN IT BE TRUE?

We can know some of the thrill of appreciating beauty in God's creation; but can we sense the greater thrill of appreciating beauty in His message of salvation?

Is the gospel abstract theology as impersonal as mathematics or chemistry? Is our acceptance of it a commitment or proposition like signing for an insurance policy?

If understood aright, it's *a message* that grips the human heart more deeply and lastingly than any human love. A heart-response to it moves one to a never-dying devotion to Christ.

Throughout the long years of her ministry Ellen White tried to awaken that heart-response in the members of the Seventh-day Adventist Church, with less than perfect success she often says. But she was overjoyed when she first heard the 1888 message. It was what she said she had been *"trying* to present" for forty-five years but had never heard anyone else publicly proclaim.[1]

It was straightforward New Testament truth but fresh to those who heard it because it was permeated with a new idea beyond what had been understood. *It linked justification by faith to the unique idea of the cosmic Day of Atonement.*

This seemed to be "new truth" rather shocking to many. Jesus said there is only one prerequisite to salvation: God loved the world, gave His only begotten Son, did all that so "who ever *believes* in Him should not perish but have everlasting life."[2] And to realize that *this* was the "third angel's message in verity," a message emphasizing grace and faith rather than beasts, a dragon, or fire and brimstone—to many it seemed strangely out of place in Adventism.

According to this, our part is to *believe* (the Greek word for believe and to have faith is the same.) Thus Jesus seems to have taught clearly

49

that salvation comes through faith, and since He added nothing else, He obviously meant that salvation comes by grace through faith alone. He didn't say it's through faith plus works.

That made many draw a deep breath. Isn't it necessary to keep the commandments, pay tithe, give offerings, keep the Sabbath, do good works? Yes, definitely; but we have no right to add to John 3:16 words that Jesus did not utter.

Then did He teach the "only believe" heresy that lulls so many people into a do-nothing-and-love-the-world, couch-potato decep- tion? Some opponents of the message mistakenly assumed that it was superficial Evangelicalism.

No; Christ taught a different kind of faith, the kind *"which works,"* and which itself produces obedience to all the commandments of God. Such faith makes the believer "zealous of good works" so numerous they cannot be measured.[3] God has already done the *loving,* and the *giving.* Our part *(believing)* comes by responding to that Good News with the heart appreciation that's appropriate— yielding to a heavenly love. Good works follow such genuine faith as surely as fruit follows seed planting. And then all the obedience part of the familiar "third angel's message" comes into place, but far more so, for here was a message that would prepare a people for the coming of Jesus. That's what alerted Ellen White.

It was and still is a mistake to assume that the 1888 message was soft on works. Pure Day-of-Atonement righteousness by faith is the only message that can produce anything other than "dead works."

Getting to Know What Faith Is

What was the measure of the Father's love? Note carefully the verb in John 3:16. He did not merely *lend* His Son; He *gave* Him.

In our human judgment it's easy to assume that the Father lent Him as a missionary or foreign diplomat who spent 33 years in lonely exile here and then returned to His heavenly home base. The agony of the cross lasted only a few hours, and the entire episode of His life on earth seems like a comparatively brief term of service. Missionaries often spend many more years in lonely service overseas.

But the reality of Christ's sacrifice means infinitely more than almost all Christians imagine. A refreshing, wider view was glimpsed by the 1888 messengers:

> Now a question: Was this a gift of only thirty-three years? ... Or was it an eternal sacrifice? ... The answer is that it was for all eternity. ... He gave himself to us. ... He bears our nature forevermore. That is the sacrifice that wins the hearts of men. ... That is the love of God. ... Whether the man believes it or not, there is a subduing power in it, and the heart must stand in silence in the presence of that awful fact. ... Ever since that blessed fact came to me that the sacrifice of the Son of God is an eternal sacrifice, and *all for me,* the word has been upon my mind almost hourly: "I will go softly before the Lord all my days."[4]

The idea is that to *believe* means to stand in awe of that sacrifice, to let your human heart be moved by it to where you forget yourself and you let that love motivate you to a measure of devotion you never dreamed possible for your selfish heart. That is how righteousness is not by faith *and* works, but by "faith *which* works."[5]

But how can we learn to appreciate that love, so that this powerful faith can begin to work in us? If we can find the answer, we can get out of our rut of lukewarmness.

Here's where the problem arose. The answer lies not in frenetic doings of this or that superficial "obedience," but in *seeing* something: *comprehending* the kind of sacrifice that Jesus made.

Paul says he "glories in the cross" because its reality solves a problem that psychiatrists and counselors are powerless to solve—the problem of deep self-centeredness. "*I* have been crucified with Christ," he says.[6] Paul is not talking about a grit-your-teeth and clench-your-fist kind of self-discipline. He saw a dynamic power in the truth of the cross that has eluded most of humanity. And because we haven't comprehended it (to borrow from Paul's prayer in Ephesians 3:14-19), we can't help but remain egocentric and lukewarm in our devotion.

What Is So Special About Jesus Dying for Us?

Billions of people have died, and many have suffered physical agony for longer periods of time than Jesus did. Is the difference only in the personhood of the Victim—He was divine (whereas we who die are human), so that His death has sufficient merit to satisfy the legal demands of the law? However true this popular doctrine may be, it does not do justice to the death of Christ. Nor does it move the human heart.

When He humbled Himself "even to the death of the cross," Christ suffered what Paul calls "the curse of the law, having become a curse for us (for it is written, 'Cursed is everyone who hangs on a tree')." The apostle is quoting the great Moses who ruled that any criminal sentenced to die on a tree is automatically "accursed of God." That is, God has slammed the door of heaven against him and refuses to hear his prayer for forgiveness.[7] Don't get hung up on whether or not this was fair; Moses said it and everybody who respected Moses believed it.

That's why a crucifixion was a gala event, like a circus. The victim is God's writeoff to be tormented as everyone's sadistic urges might dictate. If you as the spectator are "godly," you must show that you agree with God's judgment against the victim and curse him too, and do all you can to add to his torment. As Christ hung on His cross, that's how the people viewed Him. It was their duty to revile Him. He felt the "curse of God" as painfully real, and that's what killed Him.

The Bible speaks of two different kinds of death, and we must not confuse them. What we call death the Bible calls "sleep," but the real thing is "the second death."[8] It's the death in which the sufferer sees no ray of hope because he feels forever forsaken by God. It's the horror-filled realization of utter despair, of divine condemnation beyond which the sufferer can expect no vindication, no resurrection, no light beyond a never-ending midnight blackness.

More than this, it's the death wherein one feels the full weight of sin's guilt, the fires of self-condemnation and self-abhorrence burning in every cell of one's being. You have no refuge of innocence. Such a death is the "curse" that Moses had mentioned.

Since the world began, not one human soul has as yet suffered that second death, the full consciousness of that complete God-forsakenness—with the exception of Jesus. He was "made a curse for us" (KJV). He experienced to the full the feelings of depression and despair that the lost will at last sense that they brought upon themselves in the final Judgment.

Why No One Else Has Ever Died That Death

No one else has ever been physically or spiritually capable of feeling that full weight of the guilt of sin, or of sensing the glory of a forfeited heaven. There's a reason: no human being can feel this full load so long as a heavenly High Priest continues to serve as mankind's Substitute and High Priest, for "He is the propitiation ... for the sins of the whole world."[9] He took the full condemnation upon Himself, and released us ("all men") from it. This does not make "all men" to be righteous by any means; but this is why God can *treat* "all men" *as though* they were righteous. It's why God can send His rain on the just and on the unjust alike.

God has given to Seventh-day Adventists a unique insight into the nature of Christ's sacrifice. In recently rereading three major works by Evangelical scholars on the nature of *agape,* I was impressed that not one sees this insight that Ellen White and the 1888 messengers saw in the cross:

> The Saviour could not see through the portals of the tomb. Hope did not present to Him His coming forth from the grave a conqueror, or tell Him of the Father's acceptance of the sacrifice. ... Christ felt the anguish which the sinner will feel when mercy shall no longer plead for the guilty race.[10]

In Ephesians 3:14-19 we can try to measure some of the dimensions of the *agape* revealed at the cross, to sense a little of its "width and length and depth and height":

> I bow my knees to the Father of our Lord Jesus Christ, ... that He would grant you ... to be strengthened with might through His Spirit in the inner man, that Christ may dwell in your hearts through faith; that you ... may be able to comprehend with all the saints what is the width and length and depth and height— to know the love [*agape*] of Christ ... that you may be filled with all the fullness of God.

(1) Paul is not concerned about our *doing* this or that, but he prays that we might be privileged to *comprehend* something. If we grasp it, a new motivation possesses our hearts. Then all the right doings will happen. Even sacrifice will become a delight.

(2) For Christ to dwell in our hearts by faith means that we are "rooted and grounded in love [*agape*]." This is simply another way of defining faith as a heart-appreciation of that love.

(3) The dimensions of this love are as high as heaven, as deep as hell, as broad as the human race, as wide as your own heart's need (or anybody else's). It is tailor-designed to fit your own personality based on your unique life history—all the way from your conception. It's the idea in Psalm 139:

> "You have covered me in my mother's womb, …
> My frame was not hidden from You,
> When I was made in secret,
> And skillfully wrought … "

Christ being infinite, He understands the real you as no one else does, and much better than you do because you don't know that "secret" in your "mother's womb."

(4) We can't wait until eternity to begin to learn to know and appreciate what happened on the cross. It is possible now to know "by faith" what "passes knowledge." Without stretching our minds and hearts to "comprehend" it, we may find ourselves at last alienated from eternal life. Hearts can harden to a point of no return. Eternal life is not a materialistic orgy; it begins now with a new spiritual awareness. Our human hearts are so little—they need to be stretched and enlarged, as David prays, "I will run in the way of Your commandments, for You shall enlarge my heart."[11]

(5) Someone very important, even the apostle Paul, prayed for you and me that we might join "all the saints" in "comprehending" this reality. Part of the answer to Paul's prayer must have been God's sending the 1888 message to Seventh-day Adventists. It solves the problem of our universal love affair with our *ego*.

Why Has This Truth Not Been Understood as It Deserves?

Satan knows that if human beings can appreciate the dimensions of that love, they will "be filled with all the fulness of God," as Paul prays. Hence the enemy wants to eclipse or becloud it.

This has been the principal work of the "little horn" of Daniel 7 and 8 and the "beast" of Revelation 13.[12] Long before the Sabbath was changed from the seventh to the first day, this apostate power sought to corrupt the true idea of *agape* that is essential to appreciating Day-of-Atonement righteousness by faith.

Perhaps his most successful method has been to invent the doctrine of the natural immortality of the human soul. It permeates many religions. The idea came from paganism and was adopted early on by apostate Christianity. It has had a devastating effect on the true idea of the gospel, for it paralyzes it. The Seventh-day Adventist Church does not believe in that false doctrine, but the modern lukewarmness that pervades the world church comes from importing popular ideas of the gospel *that are related to it.* A few exceptions only prove the rule. For example:

(1) If the soul is naturally immortal, Christ could not have died the equivalent of "the second death." For those who accept natural immortality, His sacrifice is automatically reduced to a few hours of physical and mental suffering while He was sustained throughout by hope. Thus the pagan-papal doctrine dwarfs "the width and length and depth and height" of Christ's love. It reduces His *agape* to the dimensions of a human love motivated by self-concern and hope of reward.[13]

(2) The result is a diluting of the idea of faith. It becomes an egocentric search for security. The highest motivation possible remains *ego*-centered. All pagan religions are self-centered in their appeal, and since almost all Christian churches accept this pagan-papal doctrine, they get locked in to what is basically an egocentric mind-set. Despite their great sincerity, so long as human minds are blinded thus they cannot appreciate the dimensions of the love revealed at the cross, and in consequence are hindered from understanding the righteousness by faith idea that relates to the cleansing of the sanctuary truth.

The result has to be a widespread lukewarmness, spiritual pride, self-satisfaction, due to subservience to *ego*-centeredness. Fear always lurks beneath its surface.

(3) As best he could in his day, Luther understood this dynamic of faith as a heart-appreciation of *agape*, yet he fell short of an adequate grasp of its full dimensions because he lived too early to grasp the idea of the cleansing of the heavenly sanctuary. And after his death his followers soon reverted to the pagan-papal concept of natural immortality. Most Protestant ideas of justification by faith are therefore conditioned by this idea. A few individual exceptions prove the fact.

(4) Our 1888 message began to cut the ties that blinded us by Protestant views that beneath the surface were related to Rome. Now those ideas are bearing fruit in Protestants more and more openly leaning toward Rome. The 1888 message was "the beginning" of a rediscovery of what Paul and the apostles saw.

How the 1888 Message Was Such Unusual Good News

When Jesus died on the cross, did He make a mere *provision* whereby something *could* be done for us if we first did our part? Or did He actually *do* something for "all men"? If so, what did He do for them?

The Bible assures us that He "is the propitiation for our sins, and not for ours only but also for the whole world." As "all have sinned," so all are "being justified freely by His grace." "God was in Christ reconciling *the world* unto Himself, not imputing their trespasses to them." Since "the wages of sin is death," Jesus came that He "might taste [that] death *for every man.*" Through His "righteous act the free gift came to *all men,* resulting in justification of life."[14]

The common idea is that the sacrifice of Christ is only *provisional,* that is, it does nothing for anyone unless he first does something to activate it and "accepts Christ." As it were, Jesus stands back with His divine arms folded, doing nothing for the sinner until he decides to "accept." In other words, salvation is a heavenly process that remains inert until *we* take the initiative. Like a washing machine in a laundromat, it has been *provided,* but it does nothing for us until we first pay the price to activate it.

In contrast, the 1888 message understands our texts: (1) Christ tasted "death [the second] for every man." (2) As "all have sinned," so "all" are "being justified freely by His grace." This is a *legal* justification, as we shall soon see; He does not force anyone to become righteous against his will. (3) By virtue of Christ's sacrifice, God is not "imputing their trespasses" unto the world. He imputed them to Christ instead. This is why no lost person can suffer the second death until *after* the final judgment, which can come only after the second resurrection. And this why all can live even now, believers and unbelievers alike. Our very life is purchased by Him, even though multitudes have no knowledge of that truth. (4) "The whole world" has been redeemed, if only someone could tell them and they could believe it. Hearing and believing that truth transforms the heart.

Ellen White agrees. Every person owes his or her physical life and all he has or is to the One who "died for all":

> To the death of Christ we owe even this earthly life. . . . Never one, saint or sinner, eats his daily food, but he is nourished by the body and the blood of Christ. The cross of Calvary is stamped on every loaf. It is reflected in every water-spring.[15]

When the sinner sees this truth and his heart appreciates it, he experiences *justification by faith*. This is therefore far more than a legal declaration of acquittal—which was made at the cross for "all men." *Justification by faith includes a change of heart.* It is the same as the forgiveness that actually takes the sin away from the heart. The Greek word for forgiveness means taking it away, reclaiming *from* it.[16]

In other words, the believer who exercises such faith becomes inwardly and outwardly obedient to all the commandments of God. Such faith, if it is not hindered and confused with Babylon's error, will grow to be so mature and powerful that it will prepare a people for the return of Christ. This, said Ellen White, "is the third angel's message in verity."[17]

Not all will be saved. But the reason is deeper than that they were not clever or prompt enough to seize the initiative. That is true, but there is something beyond it. *They will have actually resisted and rejected the salvation already "freely" given them in Christ.* God has taken the initiative to save "all men," but humans have the ability, the freedom of will, to thwart and veto what Christ has already accomplished for them and has actually placed in their hands. They can repeat what Esau did who "despised" his birthright and "sold" it for "one morsel of food."[18]

We can cherish our alienation from Christ and our hatred of His righteousness until we close the gates of heaven against ourselves. According to the 1888 concept, those who are saved at last are saved due to God's initiative; those who are lost at last are lost because of their own initiative. Here is the 1888 idea:

> The faith of Christ must bring the righteousness of God, because the possession of that faith is the possession of the Lord himself. This faith is dealt to every man, even as Christ gave himself to every man. Do you ask what then can prevent every man from being saved? The answer is, Nothing, except the fact that all men will not keep the faith. If all would keep all that God gives them, all would be saved.[19]

> There is not the slightest reason why every man that has ever lived should not be saved unto eternal life, except that they would not have it. So many spurn the gift offered so freely.[20]

According to Jesus, the only sin for which anyone can be lost is that of not appreciating and receiving His grace. *This is what unbelief is.* "He who does not believe is condemned. ... And this is the condemnation, that the light has come into the world, and men *loved* darkness rather than light."[21]

How can it be that the cross is "stamped on every loaf" of bread so that even unbelieving sinners enjoy life because of Christ's sacrifice? As the Lamb "slain from the foundation of the world," He has "brought life ... to light through the gospel,"[22] life for the world itself. The human race was so degraded in the time of the Roman Empire that mankind would have destroyed themselves if Christ had not come when He did "in the fullness of the time."

Even the wicked today draw their next breath because of Christ's cross, though they do not know the fact. No one, believer or unbeliever, can know a moment's joyous laughter except that a price was paid by the One upon whom was laid "the chastisement for our peace," and by whose "stripes we are healed."[23] The Hindu doctrine of *karma* is wrong because *we* do not pay for our sins; but *Christ* paid the *karma* for them all. For "all men" He has brought "life." For those who believe, He has also brought "immortality."

Isn't Paul's Idea Clear as Sunlight?

He sets it out succinctly: "As through one man's offense judgment came to all men, resulting in condemnation, even so through one Man's righteous act, the free gift came to all men, resulting in justification of life."[24]

There are four ways that this inspired statement has been understood:

(1) The Calvinist view implies that Paul didn't say it quite right— "the free gift ... resulting in justification of life" came only on the elect, not on "all men." Or, the non-elect are so unimportant that they aren't included in "all men."

(2) The Universalist view understands from this that "all men" must be saved at last. But they err, as we shall see.

(3) Arminianism was a protest against Calvinism, but again it doesn't get what Paul actually said even though it is the generally popular Adventist view. Paul did not say it quite right—"the free gift ... resulting in justification of life" did not actually come upon "all men," says this view. Christ only made it provisional whereby it might possibly come *if, but not until,* they do something right first. Unless they activate the heavenly machinery, nothing happens. The washing machine in the laundromat is provisional, but it won't work without coins.[25] This view is widely believed, for it sounds reasonable. It superficially explains why so many will be lost—they didn't take the initiative to pay the price and put the coins in the machine. But this view conflicts with what Paul actually said and requires changing his word "gift" (repeated five times in Romans 5) into a mere "offer."

(4) The 1888 message view accepts that he said it exactly right. Christ as "the last Adam" has reversed the evil that the first Adam did. As surely as "all men" were condemned by Adam's sin, so surely "all men" have been *legally* justified by Christ's sacrifice. He has already tasted death for "every man," suffered the punishment of sin for "all men," died their second death. He is the propitiation for the sins "of

the whole world." No one could draw his next breath unless his sins had already been imputed unto Christ, for no one, saint or sinner, could bear his own full guilt even for a moment and still live.

Waggoner sees that Christ did more than make a mere *provisional plan for a possible* salvation that becomes real only *if* we succeed in taking the initiative:

> As the condemnation came upon all, so the justification comes upon all. Christ has tasted death for every man. He has given himself for all. Nay, he has given himself *to* every man. The free gift has come upon all. The fact that it is a free gift is evidence that there is no exception. If it came upon only those who have some special qualification, then it would not be a free gift. It is a fact, therefore, plainly stated in the Bible, that the gift of righteousness and life in Christ has come to every man on earth.[26]

In the light of the cross, even "neglect" of "so great salvation" is seen to be rejection of it. *This is the definition of unbelief.* Thus the lost person condemns himself before the universe. He unfits himself for eternal life. He shuts himself out of heaven.[27]

The Good News Is Better Than We Have Thought

According to the "most precious" 1888 message, our salvation does not depend on our taking the first step; it depends on our *believing* that God has taken the initiative in saving us. It does not depend on our holding on to God's hand (we are weak); it depends on our *believing* that He is holding on tight to our hand.

There is no parable that tells of a lost sheep that must find its way back to the shepherd; but there is one of a Good Shepherd who searches for His lost sheep. The ancient pagans were scandalized by the apostles' teaching that God is not waiting for man to seek Him, but is already seeking for man.[28] The lady didn't wait for her lost silver coin to come back; she went looking for it. The prodigal came home only because he remembered, and was drawn by the father's love. The initiative was always with the father; the son only responded to it.

The Bible teaches that it is not our job to initiate a "relationship" with Christ, for *He* has initiated it with us. Our job is to believe it, to cherish and appreciate it.

If teaching which professes to be righteousness by faith turns out to be a subtle works program, it nurtures lukewarmness because its bottom line is fearful self-concern. It's questionable if human wisdom can invent a righteousness by faith closer to Scripture than what Ellen White described as "most precious" which the Lord sent us "in His great mercy."

Neither is it strictly true to say that our salvation depends on our *maintaining* a relationship with the Lord. The Good Shepherd keeps looking for His sheep *"until He find it."*[29] In other words, He wants you to be saved more than you want to be saved. He does not get tired or discouraged as we do in our lukewarm unbelief.

Our salvation depends on our believing that He loves us so much that He will maintain that relationship unless we beat Him off. Stop resisting the leading and prompting of the Holy Spirit! His role is that of Husband; His people become the bride. Their devotion is always a *response* to His aggressive, initiating, and on-going love. This truth humbles the pride of man in the dust.

In other words, to put the 1888 message into very simple words— *salvation is by grace alone and receiving it depends on faith.* Your job is not to climb up to heaven or descend down to hell looking for Jesus as though He were hiding from you, but to recognize that *He has found you* by "the word of faith, which we preach."[30]

When we ask the Bible question, "What must I do to be saved?" we must let the Bible give the answer. It is not do this, and do that; get up earlier, work harder, study more; pray more; do more witnessing; make more sacrifices; give more; achieve more goals; master more techniques; go to more seminars. All these things are good, but the true answer is, *"Believe* on the Lord Jesus Christ, and you will be saved."[31]

The Bible does not teach a heresy! The key is understanding what it means to believe. Due to the natural immortality error, it is difficult for "Babylon" to grasp the idea. We can't permit Satan to preempt that genuine word "faith" through his counterfeits, so that we turn away from genuine righteousness by faith and revert to a subtle works program.

But People Still Have Problems with the Good News

Doesn't the Bible tell us that it is our job to "seek the Lord"? Do the Old Testament "seek-ye-the-Lord" texts contradict Jesus' New Testament parable of the Good Shepherd seeking us?

Even the Old Testament texts that *appear* to give that impression do not do so in context. The sin of the ancient Jews was twisting Scripture to fit their old covenant ideas. Jesus came to reveal a "grace [that] did much more abound."[32] Unless we understand we will forever wallow in a subtle form of legalism, paralyzing our message to the world so that we win only a few of those we could otherwise win.

Look at Isaiah 55:6: "Seek the Lord while He may be found, call upon Him while He is near." The Hebrew word translated "seek" (darash) does not primarily mean seek, but it means "pay attention to," or "inquire of" (compare its use in 1 Samuel 28:7).[33] Isaiah says, Pay attention to the Lord "while He is near." He emphasizes His nearness, not His farness. There is no Bible statement that reveals God as indifferently waiting for us to arouse Him from lethargy, or that He wants to hide Himself from us. Our "seeking" is always represented as a heart-response to His initiative in seeking us.

The true gospel gives a beautiful and powerful reason for serving Christ: "The love (agape) of Christ constraineth us; because we thus judge, that if one died for all, then were all dead: and that he died for all, that they which live should not henceforth live unto themselves, but unto him which died for them, and rose again."[34] The original language implies that those who sense Christ's love find it *impossible* "henceforth" to go on living for self:

> It is not the fear of punishment, or the hope of everlasting reward, that leads the disciples of Christ to follow Him. They behold the Saviour's matchless love, ... and the sight of Him attracts, it softens and subdues the soul.[35]

The pure gospel reactivated in the 1888 message provides a deep peace, and it grows in a heart that has been delivered from that subliminal fear that shadows us from the cradle to our grave.

Sometimes rage or bitterness erupts from the murky depths of our unknown selves like a volcano we thought was extinct. Molten lava pours forth from deep subterranean emotional fires.

Often they have smoldered from our infancy, yes, perhaps even from conception—like the child who realizes that he or she was the product of lust, an unwanted pregnancy. Can a fetus share somehow the bitterness of its pregnant mother? After birth the unwanted child can wonder, "Where was God when this happened?"

A child's parents may not have realized how they were destroying his or her sense of healthy self-respect by fault-finding or pressure to *earn* their love. Many of us carry a crushing load of guilt and alienation which stems from infantile traumas that are in no way our fault. Alcoholism, drug addiction, constitutional depression, sexual degradation, can often find their roots in infancy. Some say that homosexuality is triggered there.

And there are traumas of rejection that can devastate our adult lives, like the death of a spouse, or worse, divorce. Does the gospel have good news for us?

Yes—justification by faith! It gives you peace with God, as though you had never sinned *and as though no one else had ever sinned against you.* It enables you to forgive others, because you sense their guilt is corporately yours as well. It is practical healing for wounded emotions, always penetrating deeper, and blending into sanctification. And it is ministered by a High Priest who is "touched with the feeling of our infirmities."

The best modern translation of High Priest is Divine Psychiatrist or Divine Psychologist. He is on duty 24 hours a day; never takes a holiday; and He is so infinite that He gives you His full attention. You can feel like you are the only patient He has.

Chapter Five Endnotes

[1] MS. 5, 1889.

[2] John 3:16.

[3] Titus 2:14.

[4] A. T. Jones, *General Conference Bulletin,* 1895, p. 382.

[5] Galatians 5:6.

[6] Galatians 2:20.

[7] Read Philippians 2:5-8; Galatians 3:13; Deuteronomy 21:22, 23.

[8] 1 Thessalonians 4:13-15; Revelation 2:11; 20:14.

[9] 1 John 2:2.

[10] *The Desire of Ages,* p. 753; cf. *Agape and Eros* by Anders Nygren, *Testaments of Love* by Leon Morris, and *The Love Affair* by Michael Harper.

[11] Psalm 119:32.

[12] Daniel 8:9-13; 7:25; Revelation 13:1-8.

[13] See Alexander Snyman, *Natural Immortality: A Key Deception* (available from this publisher).

[14] 1 John 2:2; Romans 3:23, 24; 2 Corinthians 5:19; Hebrews 2:9; Romans 5:18.

[15] *The Desire of Ages,* p. 660.

[16] *Aphesis,* the *a* meaning "from," and *phero* meaning "carry." Cf. *Thoughts From the Mount of Blessing,* p. 114; *Selected Messages,* Book One, pp. 396, 397.

[17] This was Ellen White's phrase to describe the 1888 message. Cf. *Review and Herald,* April 1, 1890.

[18] Hebrews 12:15.

[19] E. J. Waggoner, *Signs of the Times,* January 16, 1896.

[20] *Ibid.,* March 12, 1896.

[21] John 3:17-19.

[22] Revelation 13:8; 2 Timothy 1:10.

[23] Isaiah 53:5.

[24] Romans 5:18.

[25] God's grace is indeed a provision; but grace is not *provisional.* It is freely *given* to all, not merely offered to all.

[26] *Signs of the Times,* March 12, 1896.

[27] See *The Great Controversy,* p. 543.

[28] Luke 15:3-10; 19:10; John 4:23; Romans 10:6-8, 10-13.

[29] Luke 15:4.

[30] Cf. Romans 10:6-8. All the good works will be accomplished, selflessly, by faith.

[31] Acts 16:30, 31.

[32] Exodus 21:24; Matthew 5:38-42; Romans 5:20.

[33] King Saul asks his servants to "seek" or "find" him "a woman who is a medium." This is the common word that means "seek." It is not *darash.* Next he says, "that I may go to her and *inquire* of her." That is *darash,* which is translated "seek" in Isaiah 55:6.

[34] 2 Corinthians 5:14, 15, KJV.

[35] *The Desire of Ages,* p. 480

Chapter Six

IF YOU CAN'T UNDERSTAND IT, IT'S NOT THE GOSPEL

Two opposite misunderstandings about the 1888 message try to confuse us:

(1) Many assume that it's just what they have heard all their lives from Billy Graham, and at our camp meetings or weeks of prayer. Everybody believes it and nobody seriously opposes it. Ho-hum. Why reinvent the wheel?

(2) The opposite error is to assume that because the message is different, it must be a difficult, complex theological puzzle that few can grasp.

Both ideas are mistaken. A little thought can show why.

(a) The 1888 message was "the beginning" of the latter rain and the loud cry, which was to have gone "like fire in the stubble" and in a short time lightened the earth with the glory of the closing message.[1] The final events of the prophetic scenario were at hand, with national Sunday laws and persecution imminent.[2] But now more than a century has dragged by wearily. Two World Wars and other tragedies have cursed the earth during this long delay. Something must have gone wrong. The message was indeed fresh and special. But after nearly a decade it was "in a great degree kept away" "from our people" and "from the world."[3] Meanwhile, many have assumed that our right- eousness by faith "doctrine" is the same as that of the conservative Baptists, Lutherans, or other Protestants.

But if Ellen White said it was "the third angel's message in verity," are these Sunday-keeping churches proclaiming that? Putting it all together, it seems that what we have thought is "righteousness by faith" during this more than a century has been "in a great measure" imported from the popular churches. For sure, they do not understand the third angel's message. Such importing would replace the unique concepts

65

God "sent" us in 1888. Willow Creek is just one recent example of long-lasting confusion.

(b) This chapter is to demonstrate also that (2) cannot be true. The message *is* simple; even a child can understand it. The only problem is that our deep human pride must be laid aside because genuine righteousness by faith in these last days lays "the glory of man in the dust." That includes the pride which teachers and preachers find so tempting.[4]

Our 1888 history and message remind us that "God has chosen the foolish things of the world to put to shame the wise. ... And the things which are despised God has chosen, and the things which are not, to bring to nothing the things that are, that no flesh should glory in His presence."[5] Jesus says it's only those who "hunger and thirst after righteousness [by faith]" who *can* be filled.[6]

The Basic Difference Is Motivation

There are three motives that are generally employed to lead people to become Christians:

(1) *The desire to secure a reward in heaven.* Naturally we want a place there. The motive is not evil, but neither is it lasting. Satan can find a way to make us forget. If hope of reward is the reason why we are serving Christ, the enemy can invent a temptation that overrides that desire, and we will sell out when our price gets high enough, preferring that bird-in-the-hand here and now to two-in-the-bush hereafter.

(2) *The fear of being lost in hell.* This is the other side of the same coin. It is natural also for us to be moved by this. "Through fear of death" we are "all [our] lifetime subject to bondage."[7] This motive is also not evil, but neither can it produce a Christlike character. It too will fail under strong, alluring temptation. Knowing that we have an ultimate "price," Satan can present a temptation so rooted in a more immediate fear that it will cancel out any future fear. This will at last be the "mark of the beast." There is danger that multitudes of professed Adventists will at last succumb unless they can get spiritual help.[8]

(3) *The desire for personal, social benefits here and now.* This also is natural and understandable. And if the presentation is skillful, there

can be "evangelistic success." But again, it can produce nothing more in devotion than we see in contemporary popular religion. Even if we baptize billions with this motivation, we will not hasten the coming of the Lord because it cannot prepare a people for His personal return.

The Source of Lukewarm Devotion

It is these motives that produce lukewarmness of devotion, and in the end can motivate many to sell out to our very clever enemy when he invents his final temptation. Multitudes who have heretofore appeared solid prove to be chaff.[9]

Can we not see what happens? The center of concern always remains *self,* that troublesome *ego.* "Looking to Jesus" remains tied to a radius of *ego*-concern and insecurity. Thus the deep root of fear is not cast out, only disguised.

In contrast, the motive to which the New Testament gospel appeals is a cross-inspired faith. It is a "more excellent way." Paul learned a lesson in his near-failure ministry in Athens. When he came to Corinth, he "determined not to know anything among you except Jesus Christ and him crucified." He tells the Galatians that in his preaching "Jesus Christ was clearly portrayed among you as crucified." Their response was phenomenal. As they listened, their ears were turned into eyes, and they "saw" the Son of God dying for them. This became the definition of "the hearing of faith."[10]

The apostles began with a presentation of *God's deed* in the sacrifice at the cross, not with *man's need* of personal security. Thus they could bypass the natural *ego*-centered motivations of the human heart and appeal directly to the latent sense of wonder and awe and heart-appreciation that God's *agape* arouses. A capacity for responding is built into every human soul for "God has dealt to each one a measure of faith."[11]

That "measure" (*metron,* Greek) may be illustrated by my Honda. I once bought a plain-Jane model and installed the radio myself. Although it was not then standard equipment, I was pleased to find that the Honda people had built into the car a *metron* or capacity for receiving the radio. There was an aperture provided for its installation, even holes drilled for the speakers with wires already included. No human being is born with divine love already built in—it must be imported and "installed." But God has provided the *capacity* for our learning to appreciate and receive it.

The sowing of such "hearing-of-faith" seed produced early Christians who were not lukewarm. Many sacrificed their all for Him who sacrificed His all for them, singing hymns as they went to martyrdom in the arenas. The 1888 message *began* to recover that Christ-centered motivation. It clearly differentiated between being "under the law" and "under grace."[12]

"Under the Law" vs. "Under Grace"

The usual understanding of "under the law" is "under the condemnation of the law." But to understand the meaning of the phrase we should first discover the meaning of its opposite—being "under grace."

If someone risked his life to save you from death, and you understood how much he risked for you, you would ever afterward feel under obligation *to him,* a gratitude that would motivate you to do anything you could *for him.* You would not think of *asking him* for a reward; you would want to *give him* one.

To be "under grace" is to be under a new motivation imposed by Christ's love for us. "Henceforth" we cannot stop to count the cost of sacrificing for Him nor can we ask questions about how much or how little He expects of us. Our childish questions whether this or that is a "sin that will keep us out of heaven" shrivel up into the pettiness that they are. We forget our striving for reward, for "stars in my crown," and now our concern is to help crown *Him* "King of kings and Lord of lords."

The early Christians asked, "Did the Son of God give Himself for *me,* dying like a criminal on a Roman cross, dying my second death of forsakenness by God? Oh, I must henceforth live for Him!" The result: a beautiful, unmeasured devotion devoid of egocentric legalism.

To be "under the law" is the simple opposite—to be under a sense of "I-ought-to-do-this," or "I-should-be-more-faithful," or "I should-sacrifice-more," or "I-should-stop-this-bad-habit," or "I should-read-my-Bible-more," "I-should-pray-more," etc. The rock-bottom motivation is always a fear of being lost or a hope of reward in heaven, a search for greater security here and now.

Thus the "under-the-law" motive for healthful living degenerates to a search for longer, happier life for our pleasure here and now rather than clearer minds and more healthful bodies with which to serve the One who died for us. Health reform originally came to Seventh-day Adventists as an avenue to help us appreciate what the great High Priest is accomplishing in His Most Holy Apartment ministry.

Suppose I meet an alluring temptation to commit adultery. If I say "no" because of fear of herpes or AIDS, or fear lest the pastor or church board or conference leaders hear of it, or that my wife will learn of it—I have done the right thing for the wrong reason. This would be an "under-the-law" motivation.

But if I say "no" as Joseph did in Egypt, "How can I do this great wickedness and *sin against God?*" because I can't stand the idea of bringing shame and disgrace on Christ to add to His pain—I am constrained by a new motivation; I am "under grace."

The Simplicity of Justification by Faith

If justification by faith is purely a legal pronouncement made millions of light years away that has no relation to our human heart, we verbally "accept Christ" and we start the heavenly machinery rolling. One's name is then entered in God's computer and his eternal social security benefits are *then* credited to his account. *His decision* has initiated this process of legal acquittal. He was acquisitive enough to put the coins in the washing machine. An element of pride can enter here; *he* initiated the process of his personal salvation.

But there can be no pride or "boasting" in true faith. Paul understood how we all share the guilt of "all the world," how "all have sinned," how all of us are involved in the sin of Adam—not through any "re-incarnation" but through corporate identity. "All *alike* have sinned."[13] "Death spread to all men, because all sinned." No one of us is innately better than anyone else. As all lions are by nature man-eaters, so all humans are by nature at "enmity with God," and since "whosoever hates his brother is a murderer," automatically we are all *"alike"* by nature guilty of the crucifixion of the Son of God.[14]

But there is also good news in what Paul says that at first thought looks depressing. Just as all have sinned, he continues, so all are "being justified *freely* by His grace." The heavenly machinery is *already* working, long before you make your "decision" to serve the Lord! Since the justification is "free," it must be that everyone has to be included; otherwise it could not be free.

"God set forth [Christ] to be a propitiation by His blood, ... to demonstrate ... His righteousness."[15] And note that the "blood" accomplished the propitiation, before we were born.

It doesn't make sense to say that the sacrifice of Christ *propitiates the Father,* because He already gave Christ for us. God "set forth" Christ on His cross, so that when He is "lifted up ... [He] will draw all" unto Himself by the sight of that blood.[16]

Nor does it make sense to say that the blood propitiates the devil, or buys him off. He is still our enemy. Who then is propitiated by that blood? *We* are!

This truth goes far beyond the Moral Influence Theory of the atonement because there is a solid legal basis for the atonement. Adam brought a legal condemnation on "all men;" and apart from the sacrifice of Christ, we would all be eternally lost. But Christ reversed that legal condemnation for the same "all men." That's why anyone can live!

When the sinner stops resisting and lets his proud human heart be melted by that love revealed, *justification by faith takes place.* This makes him fully obedient to the law of God. In the past, he was disobedient, and he was selfish. He still has a sinful nature and will have it until glorification, but now faith *works,* and he does not fulfill those selfish impulses. Now he is a willing slave motivated by Christ's love, and he joins Paul in saying, "The love of Christ constraineth us." *This is what it means to be "under grace."*

How the 1888 Messengers Understood Justification by Faith

(1) It makes the believer to become obedient to the law of God, not by eradicating his sinful nature but by enabling him to triumph over it:

God justifies the ungodly. … It does not mean that He glosses over a man's faults, so that he is counted righteous, although he is really wicked; but it means that He makes that man a doer of the law. The moment God declares an ungodly man righteous, that instant that man is a doer of the law. … It will be seen, therefore, that there can be no higher state than that of justification. It does everything that God can do for a man short of making him immortal, which is done only at the resurrection. … Faith and submission to God must be exercised continually, in order to retain the righteousness—in order to remain a doer of the law.[17]

The word of God which speaks righteousness has the righteousness itself in it, and as soon as the sinner believes, and receives that word into his own heart by faith, that moment he has the righteousness of God in his heart; and since out of the heart are the issues of life, it follows that a new life is thus begun in him; and that life is a life of obedience to the commandments of God.[18]

(2) *Saving faith is a heart appreciation of the sacrifice of Christ:*

In this blessed fact of the crucifixion of the Lord Jesus, which was accomplished for every soul, there is not only laid the foundation of faith for every soul, but in it there is given the *gift of faith* to every soul. And thus the cross of Christ is … the very power of God manifested to deliver us from all sin, and bring us to God.[19]

(3) *Genuine justification by faith is meaningless apart from appreciating how close Christ has come to us:*

There is no element of weakness in the law; the weakness is in the flesh. It is not the fault of a good tool that it cannot make a sound pillar out of a rotten stick. … Poor, fallen man had no strength resting in his flesh to enable him to keep the law. And so God imputes to believers the righteousness of Christ, who was made in the likeness of sinful flesh, so that "the righteousness of the law" might be fulfilled in their lives. ... Christ took upon Himself man's nature, and will impart of His own righteousness to those who accept His sacrifice.[20]

(4) *This special, unique message was intended by the Lord to prepare His people for translation:*

> What means, then, this special message of justification that God has been sending these [seven] years to the church and to the world [1895]? ... This special message of justification which God has been sending us is to prepare us for glorification at the coming of the Lord. In this, God is giving to us the strongest sign that it is possible for Him to give, that the next thing is the coming of the Lord.[21]

But now a question arises. When the 1888 messengers said that justification by faith makes the believer "a doer of the law," did they inadvertently fall into the error of the Roman Catholic view which says that justification is "making righteous"? No, the two views are as different as night and day:

(1) The Catholic view sees justification administered exclusively by the Catholic Church through its sacraments: "The instrumental cause is the sacrament of baptism." "The sacrament of Penance" is necessary to be administered by the same Church. Also, "sacramental confession, ... sacerdotal absolution," "fasts, alms, prayers, and the other pious exercises" are needed.[22] In contrast, the 1888 message teaches justification by faith in Christ alone, and the instrumentality is the Holy Spirit, not a church or hierarchy.

(2) The Catholic view denies that the sacrifice of Christ "restored the whole race of men to favor with God."[23] "Though He died for all, yet do not all receive the benefit of his death, but those only unto whom the merit of his passion is communicated" by the sacraments of the Church.[24] In contrast, the 1888 message caught the apostles' Good News that *legally* "all ... [are] justified freely by his grace through the redemption that is in Christ Jesus;" "through one Man's righteous act the free gift came to all men, resulting in justification of life;" "He Himself is the propitiation for our sins, and not for ours only but also for the

whole world;" "the Lamb of God ... takes away the sin of the world!"[25] Even Luther and Calvin came short of powerfully articulating this larger New Testament vision of what Christ accomplished on His cross.

(3) In Roman Catholic justification, the sinner is not united to Christ through faith by the free imputation of the whole of Christ's righteousness, but God gradually infuses his soul with an inherent righteousness that is meritorious, so that persevering Catholics will "have truly merited eternal life ... if so be, however, that they depart in grace."[26] The 1888 message recognizes that the believer never has had or will have an iota of merit in himself, nor any righteousness inherent in himself; righteousness is only *in Christ* and the believer receives it only *through faith*.

(4) The Council of Trent taught that "adults ... may ... convert themselves to their own justification, by freely assenting to and cooperating with that said grace." This "anticipated ... grace of God" *precedes* justification and requires first a "disposition, or, preparation, [which] is followed by justification itself." The Trent Chapters VI and VII list many items of "preparation" that the sinner must do *before* he can be justified, "things which precede justification."[27]

The 1888 message recognized that man has no part whatever in his justification and can make no preparation for it or do anything to "precede" it. It is done wholly by Christ, and all the believer can do is to receive, accept, believe, appreciate, what Christ accomplished, and stop hindering this dynamic faith to work obedience by love.

(5) The Catholic view encourages doubt and fear: "Each one, when he regards himself, and his own weakness and indisposition, may have fear and apprehension touching his own grace; seeing that no one can know with a certainty of faith, which can not be subject to error, that he has obtained the grace of God." "If any one saith, that it is necessary for every one, for the obtaining of remission of sins, that he believe for certain ... that his sins are forgiven him: let him be anathema."[28] The 1888 message recognized that "unto every one of us is given grace according to the measure of the gift of Christ." The message encourages complete confidence in God's gift of that grace.[29]

(6) The Catholic view fails to see that the whole fallen human race which is "in Adam" is corporately "in Christ" by virtue of His sacrifice. The 1888 message sees sin as a continual, unbelieving resistance of

Christ who "will draw all men unto Me" if they will stop resisting. Christ has already tasted the second death for everyone, and thus no one can suffer at last for his sins unless he persists in unbelief, disbelieves, and rejects what Christ has done for him.[30]

(7) Thus the Catholic Church still in principle denies that justification is by faith alone. When they say that justification "makes righteous," their idea is opposed to that of the 1888 message. Catholic "justification" is infused, inherent, and meritorious, and not solely of faith: "No one ought to flatter himself up with faith alone, fancying that by faith alone he is made an heir, and will obtain the inheritance."[31]

The 1888 message broke through centuries of Catholic and Protestant fog into a clearer view of the sunlit New Testament truth.

How Good News Permeated the 1888 Message

A so-called "gospel" without Good News has to be a counterfeit. The burden of the apostles' message is "glad tidings."[32] This gave people no false assurance. The burden of their message was how faithful God is.[33] Thus the people "received the atonement," or reconciliation, with God.[34]

Man's problem is our alienation from God due to our guilt and distorted view of His character. Troubles and disappointments arouse bad feelings. Why doesn't He do more to help us? Why does He permit suffering?[35]

Paul pleaded, "Be reconciled to God." Believe the truth about His character, and let your enmity be healed and your guilt be taken away.[36] Then faith can go to work, producing works of righteousness in the life. This welcome "glad tidings" was the burden of the 1888 message:

Let the weary, feeble, sin-oppressed souls take courage. Let them 'come boldly unto the throne of grace,' where they are sure to find grace to help in time of need, because that need is felt by our Saviour in the very time of need. … The very temptation that presses you touches Him. His wounds are ever fresh, and He ever lives to make intercession for you.

What wonderful possibilities there are for the Christian! To what heights of holiness he may attain! No matter how much Satan may war against him, assaulting him where the flesh is weakest, he may abide under the shadow of the Almighty, and be filled with the fullness of God's strength.[37]

Why is it that the sun does not slip out of his place? ... The "powerful word" of Jesus Christ holds the sun there, and causes him to go on in his course. And *that same power* is to hold up *the believer in Jesus.*[38]

There is special good news included in forgiveness. We gain very little self-respect in being merely pardoned at no expense to God. If all God does for us is to pardon or excuse our sins, we still carry the pollution deep within our souls.

But the "blood of the new covenant ... is shed for many for the *remission* of sins," taking them away. Sins are to be "blotted out." True forgiveness will do more than pardon us, because we at last realize what it cost Him. It will "cleanse us from all unrighteousness."[39] Says the 1888 idea:

When Christ covers us with the robe of His own righteousness, He does not furnish a cloak for sin, but takes the sin away. And this shows that the forgiveness of sins is something more than a mere form, something more than a mere entry in the books of record in heaven, to the effect that the sin has been canceled. The forgiveness of sins is a reality, ... something that vitally affects the individual. It actually clears him from guilt; and if he is cleared from guilt, is justified, made righteous, he has certainly undergone a radical change.[40]

Ellen White agrees:

God's forgiveness is not merely a judicial act by which He sets us free from condemnation. It is not only forgiveness *for* sin, but reclaiming *from* sin.[41]

Good News: A People Can Actually Be Prepared for Christ's Coming

There is a true aspect of Adventism which has been widely opposed in recent years. The very possibility of a people overcoming so that they might be ready for Christ's coming has been muted, denied, and even ridiculed. It has often been denounced as the heresy of "perfectionism."

But the Bible is clear: "The grace of God that brings salvation has appeared to all men. It teaches us to say 'No' to ungodliness and worldly passions, and to live self-controlled, upright and godly lives in this present age, while we wait for the blessed hope—the glorious appearing of our great God and Savior, Jesus Christ, who gave himself for us to redeem us from all wickedness and to purify for himself a people that are his very own, eager to do what is good." Revelation complements this "blessed hope" by describing a people who "follow the Lamb wherever He goes. … They are blameless."[42]

Scripture teaches that those who look "for that blessed hope" will truly, not supposedly, "keep the commandments of God, and the faith of Jesus."[43] The 1888 message does not deserve ridicule. This glorious result will be accomplished through righteousness by faith, not through an *ego*-centered works program:

> God manifest in the flesh, God manifest in sinful flesh, is the mystery of God—not God manifested in sin*less* flesh, but in sin*ful* flesh. That is to say, … God will so dwell yet in sinful flesh today that in spite of all the sinfulness of sinful flesh, his influence, his glory, his righteousness, his character, shall be manifested wherever that person goes. … In Christ is shown the Father's purpose concerning us. All that was done in Christ was to show what will be done in us. … Is it too much, then, for us to think that sinful flesh, such as we; worthless dust and ashes, as are we—is it too much for us to think that such as we can manifest the glory of the Lord, which is refracted through Jesus Christ,—the glory of the Lord shining from the face of Jesus Christ? … It is our part to furnish a place for the glory to fall, that it may shine in the beautiful reflected rays of the glory of God.[44]

Tucked away in an obscure text of the Bible is a Good News promise that cannot fail to be fulfilled: "Unto two thousand and three hundred days; then shall the sanctuary be cleansed."[45] Amplified and complemented by the message of Hebrews in the New Testament, this prophecy describes the special work of the heavenly High Priest on this cosmic Day of Atonement. Today we are living "in the days of the seventh angel, when he shall begin to sound."[46] This is the work which began in 1844.

Our friends in other churches are sincere, warm-hearted Christians living up to all the light they have. Lutheran, Calvinist, Methodist, Baptist, Pentecostal, or whatever, their "righteousness by faith" sincerely knows nothing of the cleansing of the heavenly sanctuary, nothing of an antitypical Day of Atonement. The idea of a special heart-preparation for the return of Christ is dimly, if at all, comprehended.

The Seventh-day Adventist 1888 message sees a successful resolving of the "great controversy between Christ and Satan." The Lord finds a people willing to cooperate fully with Him in the last days. Christ as heavenly High Priest cleanses His sanctuary. It's not our job to do it.

Our part is to cooperate with Him, to *let Him do it*, to stop hindering Him.

Chapter Six Endnotes

[1] *Review and Herald,* November 22, 1892; *Selected Messages,* Book One, p. 118.
[2] See *Seventh-day Adventist Encyclopedia,* article "Sunday Laws," p. 1273.
[3] Cf. *Selected Messages,* Book One, pp. 234, 235.
[4] Cf. *Christ Our Righteousness,* p. 104.
[5] 1 Corinthians 1:27-29.
[6] Matthew 5:6.
[7] Hebrews 2:15.
[8] "The shaking of God blows away multitudes like dry leaves." *Testimonies,* Vol. 4, p. 89.
[9] Cf. *Testimonies,* Vol. 5, p. 81.
[10] 1 Corinthians 2:1-4; Galatians 3:1-5.
[11] Romans 12:3.
[12] Romans 6:14, 15.
[13] Romans 3:19, 23, NEB; 5:12.
[14] 1 John 3:15.
[15] Romans 3:25.
[16] John 12:32.
[17] E. J. Waggoner, *Signs of the Times,* May 1, 1893.
[18] Waggoner, *The Gospel in Creation,* p. 28.
[19] A. T. Jones, *Review and Herald,* October 24, 1899.
[20] Waggoner, *Bible Echo,* February 15, 1892. More about this in a later chapter.
[21] Jones, *General Conference Bulletin,* 1895, p. 367.
[22] Council of Trent, Sixth Session, Chapter VII; Chapter XIV. From Philip Schaff, The *Creeds of Christendom,* Vol. 11, pp. 89-118.
[23] *Selected Messages,* Book One, p. 343.
[24] Trent, Chapter III.
[25] Romans 3:24; 5:18; 1 John 2:2; John 1:29.
[26] Trent, Chapter XVI.
[27] Chapter V; Chapter VII; Chapter VIII.
[28] Chapter IX; Canon XIII.
[29] Ephesians 4:7.
[30] John 12:32, KJV; Hebrews 2:9; John 3:17, 18; cf. *Steps to Christ,* p. 27.
[31] Trent, Chapter XI.
[32] See Acts 13:32-34.
[33] See Romans 8:26-39, for example.
[34] Romans 5:11.
[35] The answer has to be that God suffers with us, "in Christ." More than we do, He longs to bring this world's suffering to an end. But first He must have a people who have received a final atonement, who have ceased resisting His grace, who can proclaim a message that lightens the earth with glory.
[36] 2 Corinthians 5:20.
[37] Waggoner, *Christ and His Righteousness,* p. 30.
[38] Jones, *General Conference Bulletin,* 1893, p. 218.
[39] Matthew 26:28; Acts 2:38; 3:19; 1 John 1:9; 2:1, 2.
[40] Waggoner, *Christ and His Righteousness,* p. 66.
[41] *Thoughts from the Mount of Blessing,* p. 114.
[42] Titus 2:11-14; Revelation 14:4, 5, NIV.
[43] Revelation 14:12.
[44] Jones, *General Conference Bulletin,* 1893, pp. 377-380.
[45] Daniel 8:14, KJV.
[46] Revelation 10:7, KJV; see Hebrews 8, 9, 10.

Chapter Seven

CAN THE GOOD NEWS BE MADE TOO GOOD?

Jesus promises, "Go into all the world and preach the gospel to every creature.... And these signs will follow those who believe: In My name they will cast out demons; they will speak with new tongues [languages, Greek]; they will take up serpents; and if they drink anything deadly, it will by no means hurt them; they will lay hands on the sick, and they will recover."[1]

Matthew gives another version of the same assurance of success: "All authority has been given to Me in heaven and on earth. Go therefore, and make disciples of all nations. ... And lo, I am with you always, even to the end of the age."

And John adds what he remembers hearing the Lord say, which is even more astounding: "He who believes in Me, the works that I do he will do also; and greater works than these he will do, because I go to My Father."[2]

Are these promises too good to be true?

They will be fulfilled, without fanaticism and without extremism, in the final message proclaimed by the fourth angel of Revelation 18:1-4. If the Bible is true, the whole world is to be "illuminated" with the glory of a powerful message. It must penetrate to Hindu, Muslim, Buddhist thinking, as well as that of professed Christians. Everyone.

The key to the fulfillment is in two significant phrases: (1) a people must be prepared to "preach the *gospel*," and (2) the fulfillment will come through those "who *believe* in Me." Only "the gospel of Christ ... is the power of God to salvation for everyone who believes." In other words, there is tremendous power in the message of true righteousness by faith.

But the devil makes a specialty of telling us that this news is too good to be true. And it seems easy to doubt.

What's Going On Behind the Scenes?

Moral and spiritual plagues afflict society, drug abuse, alcoholism, marital infidelity, sexual immorality, corruption, compulsive eating disorders, widespread psychological depression. A steady and increasing deterioration of the human spirit is bringing millions to the place where they seem mentally unable even to comprehend Christ's everlasting gospel in the third angel's message.

Meanwhile God has instructed "four angels" to "hold" the "four winds" of human passion "till we have sealed the servants of our God."[3] You couldn't drive to church safely, otherwise! Thank God the Holy Spirit is still working.

The sealing is obviously the final work to be accomplished by the gospel. The loosing of the "four winds" will be the complete breakdown of social order, decency, morality, fidelity, including economic and political security. The Bible says it will be "Babylon" dropping into the sea "like a millstone"—the end of weddings, Christmases, Easters, shopping malls, sports, materialistic orgies, vacations, and yes, of sensuality.

If the special message which the three angels of Revelation 14 proclaim is "the everlasting gospel" in the setting of the Day of Atonement, then it is obvious that the gospel cannot be clearly understood except in the context of the cleansing of the sanctuary. Ellen White has reminded us of this significance:

> The third angel closes his message thus: "Here is the patience of the saints; here are they that keep the commandments of God, and the faith of Jesus." As he repeated these words, he pointed to the heavenly sanctuary. The minds of all who embrace this message are directed to the most holy place, where Jesus stands before the ark, making His final intercession for all those for whom mercy still lingers, and for those who have ignorantly broken the law of God.[4]

The ministry of the great High Priest in the *first* apartment (the first phase of His sanctuary atoning ministry) prepares believers for death. And that is a marvelous work. The ministry in the *second* apartment (or phase) is specifically to prepare a corporate body of God's people for translation *without seeing death*.

The Point is Simple

If His people will faithfully proclaim that sealing message, the Lord has promised that He will do His part to restrain the exploding evil in the world until giving the message is completed. But if the church does not faithfully proclaim the message that alone can prepare a people for the return of Christ, He cannot hold in check those near-exploding global forces of evil. Merely to proclaim a message that prepares people for death is no longer good enough. The time must come when there is a message that prepares a people for His second coming.

This gets pretty serious.

Surely it was never His will that World Wars I and II should unleash such havoc and pain in the world, as well as the horrors and violence that are so common in many lands today. The world has been starving for "the third angel's message in verity," and still is. We can be perilously close to economic, political, and social ruin.

God's plan was that a small people would make a great impact on world consciousness by proclaiming a unique message that Heaven could fully endorse. They would be like little David with five smooth stones facing Goliath, and they would be as successful. The gospel power to prevent those tornadoes of passion was to be in the message itself, not in impressive church institutions, budgets, or organization.

Even today, over a century later, those who study the 1888 message realize its built-in "heavenly credentials" that convince both honest Adventists and non-Adventists.

Speaking of power, there are also in the world numerous "faith-healers," charismatics, and charlatans who prey upon people's self-centered motivations. Many profess the name of Christ, but there is a problem which is stated clearly by Ellen White:

They can see no light in the third angel's message, which shows the way into the most holy place, ... and they can not be benefited by the intercession of Jesus there. Like the Jews, who offered their useless sacrifices, they offer up their useless prayers to the apartment which Jesus has left; and Satan, pleased with the deception, assumes a religious character, and leads the minds of these professed Christians to himself, working with his power, his signs and lying wonders, to fasten them in his snare.[5]

We are told that Satan can work miracles and even give his followers "light and much power, but no sweet love, joy, and peace."[6] But there is Good News lurking beneath this shadowed truth. *The presence of the counterfeit only proves that the genuine is in existence somewhere.*

How a Pure Gospel Message Does Have Power

Everywhere the early apostles preached, something happened. No one could sit on the fence after listening to them.[7] The reason they turned "the world upside down" was not their cleverness or their personalities. The power was in the content of their message.

Peter's sermon at Pentecost reveals the source of their power: they understood our involvement in crucifying Christ. All the Gentile world, not just the Jewish leaders, were seen to be guilty of the rejection and murder of the Son of God. Pentecost was corporate guilt exposed. Enmity against God had blossomed into the supreme crime of eternity. The apostles minced no words in telling it.[8] That revelation catalyzed humanity. Two classes emerged: those who hated the truth, and those who rejoiced for it. No one sat on the fences.

Ellen White declared that the 1888 message was the beginning of the *latter* rain. But there is a profound truth hidden in this history: it was not the works of men or the supposed revival of the church in the early 1890s that began to fulfill that wondrous prophecy; it was the message itself—"the revelation of the righteousness of Christ, the sin-pardoning Redeemer."[9] There was in it "the truth of the gospel," the most powerful force that can be exerted on human hearts.[10] And once more, had the message been accepted and proclaimed, the world would again have been catalyzed into two groups: those who hated the truth and would enforce the mark of the beast, and those who would receive the seal of God.

Some of the human problems which the apostles' gospel solved were the same that perplex social scientists today. Miracles took place at Corinth that were greater than mere physical healings: "Neither fornicators, nor idolaters, nor adulterers, nor homosexuals, nor sodomites, nor thieves, nor covetous, nor drunkards, nor revilers, nor extortioners will inherit the kingdom of God. And such were some of you. But you were washed, but you were sanctified, but you were justified in the name of the Lord Jesus and by the Spirit of our God."[11]

These Same Problems Afflict the Human Race Today

They are not merely occasional moral lapses. Compulsive obsessions or addictions have roots going down to people's toes. How were those problems solved in Corinth? The answer is in the text: *by the message of justification by faith.*

There was frightful moral depravity then. Citizens and slaves were so violently cruel that they reveled in watching human beings fight wild animals, and each other, to the death. The more blood the more fun. Prostitution was sanctified as a part of religion. But through the proclamation of the gospel, "grace did much more abound" and reigned "through righteousness [by faith] unto eternal life."[12] The story of the cross touched secret springs hidden deep in Gentile and Jewish human hearts, and released latent abilities undreamed of.

The message placed "under grace" people who were shackled by all kinds of compulsive sin, including that of "abusers of themselves with mankind." Now a new compulsion of love shackled them willingly and gladly to Christ. The result: a happy one. "Sin shall not have dominion over you," said Paul, "for you are not under law but under grace."[13]

Even today, that message of grace conquers all kinds of secret addictions when appeals to self-centered concern are helpless to motivate people to a true and lasting change.

What Truth Does a Message of Grace Emphasize?

The apostles' message of grace proclaimed what is often neglected or denied within the church today—the reality of Christ's human nature being *like,* not *unlike,* ours. What impressed those people was the Son of God coming "nigh at hand," taking their nature, being tempted as they were, suffering in their place, accepting their poverty that He might give them His wealth, conquering their temptations by faith but with the same "equipment" of nature they had. Paul reminded the Corinthians of what they had learned from him: "You know the grace of our Lord Jesus Christ, that though He was rich, yet for your sakes He became poor, that you through His poverty might become rich."[14]

Here was a power that gripped human hearts as nothing had done in all previous history. The most hopeless captives found deliverance. The cross-reality burned its way into the deepest recesses of thinking, as a spiritual catharsis. A new sense of self-respect emerged that nothing could destroy.

The Power in the 1888 Message

For a brief time after the Minneapolis Conference, the precious message was proclaimed with similar results in our camp meetings and schools. What were its fruits? Ellen White said: "The present message—justification by faith—is a message from God; it bears the divine credentials, for its fruit is unto holiness."[15] There seems to have been something phenomenal about it:

I have never seen a revival work go forward with such thoroughness, and yet remain so free from all undue excitement. There was no urging or inviting. The people were not called forward, but there was a solemn realization that Christ came not to call the righteous, but sinners, to repentance. ... We seemed to breathe in the very atmosphere of heaven.[16]

I saw that the power of God attended the message wherever it was spoken. You could not make the people believe in South Lancaster that it was not a message of light that came to them. ... God has set His hand to do this work. We labored in Chicago; it was a week before there was a break in the meetings. But like a wave of glory, the blessing of God swept over us as we pointed men to the Lamb of God that taketh away the sin of the world. The Lord revealed His glory, and we felt the deep movings of His Spirit.[17]

Note that it was not the speakers, hierarchical pressure, promotional strategies, or advertising, that had such power." *It was in the message itself.*

Has this "most precious message" been clearly proclaimed to the world since then, so that the final sealing work could be done?

The obvious fact of over a hundred years of history since the loud cry "began" seems significant. If the message had been truly proclaimed, Christ would have come. It's that simple. Ellen White boldly says that "in a great measure" it has been "kept away" from both the church and the world.[18]

But there is good news—to discover the reason for the long delay of over a century has to give us hope. It is in our power to recover the message because the same "Lord [who] in His great mercy sent" it has provided for its being available in out-of-print books and periodicals for us to see today. If He "sent" it through "His special messengers" who were given "heavenly credentials," it makes very good sense to see what they had to say.

What Plan Does God Have for His Remnant Church?

The heart of God yearns for all the heart-burdened captives of Satan in the world today. Christ paid the price for their deliverance, and yet millions, yes, billions, are virtually ignorant of His work as High Priest in the Most Holy Apartment. He must depend on His church to proclaim and to demonstrate that unique message which alone can deliver from Satan's grip.

He has promised that His remnant church is to be the avenue through which His much more abounding grace is to be communicated to the world. No off-shoot can succeed. There is a grace greater than can be understood by any people who have no knowledge of the Most Holy Apartment ministry:

It shall come to pass afterward [in the last days] that I will pour out My Spirit on all flesh.... And it shall come to pass that whoever calls on the name of the Lord shall be saved. For in Mount Zion and in Jerusalem there shall be deliverance, as the Lord has said, among the remnant whom the Lord calls.[19]

The earth will be filled with the knowledge of the glory of the Lord, as the waters cover the sea.[20]

I saw another angel coming down from heaven, having great authority, and the earth was illuminated with his glory. ... And I heard another voice from heaven saying, "Come out of her [Babylon], my people, lest you share in her sins, and lest you receive of her plagues."[21]

Note that word, "having great *authority.*" In the original language it is the same word that Jesus used when He told His disciples that "all authority has been given to Me in heaven and on earth." Now, in His closing work of atonement, He is finally able to communicate that "authority" through His people on earth. Now at last through His name they will be empowered to do the "greater works" than He did on earth.

Is the Prophecy Too Good to be True?

Ellen White says it will happen:

In visions of the night representations passed before me of a great reformatory movement among God's people. Many were praising God. The sick were healed, and other miracles were wrought. A spirit of intercession was seen, even as was manifested before the great day of Pentecost. Hundreds and thousands were seen visiting families. ... Hearts were convicted by the power of the Holy Spirit, and a spirit of genuine conversion was manifest. On every side doors were thrown open to the proclamation of the truth. The world seemed to be lightened with the heavenly influence.[22]

People thought Paul was beside himself in his unmeasured devotion to Christ. He replied that it was not because he was made of more heroic stuff than others. Christ's love at the cross "constrained" him. That is, it motivated him, pushed him forward relentlessly, almost in spite of himself. Now he found it impossible to go on living for self. It made him a "new creation." To be reconciled to God, to have the psychic barrier removed that had beclouded his soul all his life, was totally joyous. The cross captured him forever, and he begs us not to look at it and yawn in boredom: "We then, as workers together with Him also plead with you not to receive the grace of God in vain."[23]

Says one of the messengers:

We "live by the faith of the Son of God, who loved me, and gave himself for me." Gal. 2:20. O, he loved me! When he gave himself in all his glory, and all his wondrous worth for me, who was nothing, is it much that I should give myself to him?[24]

Let us try to immerse ourselves in Paul's message of grace so that we can feel those waves rolling over us.

For the promise that he would be the heir of the world was not to Abraham or to his seed through the law, but through the righteousness of faith. … It is of faith that it might be according to grace, so that the promise might be sure to all … those who are of the faith of Abraham, who is the father of us all. …

Through our Lord Jesus Christ … we have access by faith into this grace in which we stand. … The grace of God and the gift by the grace of the one Man, Jesus Christ, abounded to many. … Those who receive abundance of grace and of the gift of righteousness will reign in life through the One, Jesus Christ. … Where sin abounded, grace abounded much more, so that as sin reigned in death, even so grace might reign through righteousness to eternal life through Jesus Christ our Lord. …

Shall we continue in sin that grace may abound? Certainly not! How shall we who died to sin live any longer in it? …

Sin shall not have dominion over you, for you are … under grace.[25]

Note what this treasure-laden-passage says:
(1) Righteousness by faith is not cold theology. It is the day-by-day practical-godliness ministry of grace.
(2) Faith provides access into this grace which opens the gates to

hope and glory. One's self-respect goes up to ten when you understand the gospel.

(3) "The gift by the grace … abounded to many." "In the matchless gift of His Son, God has encircled the whole world with an atmosphere of grace as real as the air which circulates around the globe. All who choose to breathe this life-giving atmosphere will live, and grow up to the stature of men and women in Christ Jesus."[26] Walk outdoors and fill your lungs with fresh air; then ask: could you get more if you were the only person on earth? And then look at all those we-thought-wicked-people breathing their fill of the same "atmosphere of grace." Who knows who of them will respond at last?

(4) Grace is greater than our sin (that is stupendous!). Hard as it is to believe, believe it.

(6) Grace abounding makes it *impossible* for the believer to continue living in sin. Obsessions, captivity to evil habits, alienations, are disarmed.

(7) Grace thus imposes a new captivity which is an unending motivation to holiness of life.

How Can You Be Sure That You Are Included?

Not one human soul in all the world is left out.

The grace of God that brings salvation has appeared to all men. It teaches us to say "No" to ungodliness and worldly passions, and to live self-controlled, upright and godly lives in this present age, while we wait for the blessed hope—the glorious appearing of our great God and Savior, Jesus Christ, who gave himself for us to redeem us from all wickedness and to purify for himself a people that are his very own, eager to do what is good.[27]

To each one of us grace was given according to the measure of Christ's gift.[28]

In short:

(1) The Holy Spirit imparts to "all men" an intruding sense of the kindness and mercy of God, knocking for entrance to all despairing

worldly hearts. Listen, look, don't slam the door. Pause to appreciate that grace, and you will find yourself beginning to cherish it.

(2) There is an insight here that the Supreme Court needs to see. Much as we may excuse ourselves by thinking that addictions to alcohol, drugs, or lust are merely a "disease," *they are in reality volitional.* The problem is that the human will is held captive. But the grace of Christ actually teaches us *how* to exercise a *controlling* volition, *how* to "say 'No'" to impulses to evil. Granted, it sounds like a truism, but nevertheless it's true.

No addict in all the world faces a more terrible compulsion than Jesus felt as He knelt in Gethsemane and prayed, "O My Father, if it is possible, let this cup pass from Me; nevertheless, not as I will, but as You will."[29] And a few hours later, the compulsive temptation to come down from the cross and abandon His suffering was even stronger; *no one has ever felt such tugging at the soul.*

(3) When the grace of God teaches us also to say what Jesus said to temptation—"No"—this is not a vain choice. When *grace* teaches us to say that powerful word, the result is guaranteed. We henceforth "live self-controlled, upright and godly lives in this present age" even with alluring temptations all around. It would be no great achievement to live such lives in perfect surroundings, but Paul adds that God's great salvation is demonstrated in a *wicked* world, as wicked as the one that crucified the Son of God.

However, saying "No!" would be vain if the motivation is egocentric. That's why in a previous presidential administration Nancy Reagan's popular "say no" campaign was so fruitless in solving the national drug problem. Only when *"grace* teaches us to say 'No'" does the volition become a sanctified, successful one.

(4) This deliverance by grace fills the heart with "the blessed hope" of seeing Jesus face to face at His return. Paul's righteousness by faith is Adventist to the core, and the core of Adventism is the message of the cross of Christ in the light of the Day of Atonement.

(5) Thus the secret of this marvelous power is in that sacrifice where He "gave Himself for us," His truth penetrating deeper than all the psychiatry in the world in probing the source of our sin and alienation.

(6) The Savior does a good job when He saves; no lingering root of "wickedness" left in the heart to produce a future fall from grace.

Do you want to be like Jesus? Then receive the grace that he has so fully and so freely given. Receive it in the measure in which *he has given it,* not in the measure in which you think you deserve it. Yield yourself to it, that it may work in you and for you the wondrous purpose for which it is given, and it will do it. It will make you like Jesus.[30]

Salvation from sin certainly depends upon there being more power in grace than there is in sin. ... Wherever the power of grace can have control, it will be just as easy to do right as without this it is easy to do wrong.

No man ever yet naturally found it difficult to do wrong ... because man naturally is enslaved to a power—the power of sin—that is absolute in its reign.... But let a mightier power than that have sway, then ... it will be just as easy to serve the will of the mightier power.

But grace is not simply more powerful than sin.... There is much more power in grace than there is in sin. ... Just so much more hope and good cheer there are for every sinner in the world.[31]

Is All This Too Good To Be True?

Beware lest you let yourself think so, for it is dangerous to doubt how good the Good News is.

Chapter Seven Endnotes

1 Mark 16:15, 17, 18.
2 Matthew 28:18-20; John 14:12.
3 Revelation 7:1-4; *Early Writings,* pp. 36-38.
4 *Early Writings,* p. 254.
5 *Ibid.,* p. 261.
6 *Ibid.,* pp. 55, 56.
7 See for example, Acts 17:1-6.
8 Acts 2:23-37.
9 *Review and Herald,* November 22, 1892.
10 Cf. Galatians 2:14.
11 1 Corinthians 6:9-11.
12 Romans 5:20, 21.
13 *Ibid.,* 6:14.
14 2 Corinthians 8:9.
15 *Review and Herald,* September 3, 1889.
16 *Ibid.,* March 5, 1889.
17 *Ibid.,* March 18, 1890.
18 *Selected Messages,* Book One, pp. 234, 235.
19 Joel 2:28, 32; Acts 2:17.
20 Habakkuk 2:14.
21 Revelation 18:1, 4.
22 *Testimonies,* Vol. 9, p. 126.
23 2 Corinthians 5:14-6:1.
24 A. T. Jones, *General Conference Bulletin,* 1895, p. 351.
25 Romans 4:13, 16; 5:2, 15, 17, 20, 21; 6:1, 14, 15.
26 *Steps to Christ,* p. 68.
27 Titus 2:11-14, NIV.
28 Ephesians 4:7.
29 Matthew 26:39.
30 Jones, *Review and Herald,* April 17, 1894.
31 Jones, *ibid.,* September 1, 1896.

Chapter Eight

THE 1888 MESSAGE AND CHASTITY: THE "PRECIOUS" NEARNESS OF OUR SAVIOR

A prominent part of the 1888 message was the refreshing idea that in His incarnation the Son of God came close to us. It was new to many because Roman Catholic and most Protestant leaders of the era held that Christ was "exempt" from inheriting our fallen, sinful nature. Inevitably the idea had to be that He is far away from us; He belongs in stained glass windows in the cathedrals. The bottom line gets through in a subtle way: real obedience to God's holy law is virtually impossible for those who have a fallen, sinful nature (all of us).

Jones and Waggoner both believed that the idea that Christ was so "exempt" was a legacy of Roman Catholicism on the same level as Sunday-keeping and natural immortality, both of which Protestantism generally accepted. The two "messengers" "the Lord sent" saw that the idea was a virtual denial of the biblical truths of righteousness by faith.

Why was the subject so important in their thinking? They related it to the unique Adventist idea of the cleansing of the heavenly sanctuary. The cleansing of the "books of record" in heaven cannot take place until first a cleansing work is accomplished in the hearts of God's people on earth.[1] The Good News is that a final and total reconciliation with God must and will take place, which of course means a final and total heart-reconciliation with the holy law of God.

That final atonement is not a works trip, but a faith experience. It is a by-faith-identification with Christ so complete that those who believe will "overcome even as [He] overcame."[2] And right here was where the truth of the nature of Christ came into focus.

Christ "overcame" by taking on His sinless nature our fallen, sinful nature and therein "condemning sin in the flesh," the same fallen sinful flesh that all mankind possess. It was a mighty accomplishment. The two messengers saw that only with that "faith *of* Jesus" will it be possible for a people to meet the final tests and be ready for His coming. Thus their understanding of Christ in His incarnation was uniquely "adventist."

A careful reading of Ellen White's some 300 plus expressions of endorsement of their message makes clear that she was heartily in support of their convictions.

The Savior Who Came All the Way to Where We Are

When Jones and Waggoner ministered to the teachers and students at South Lancaster just after the Minneapolis Conference in early 1889, Ellen White reported what impressed her about the message of her two young colleagues:

> On Sabbath afternoon, many hearts were touched, and many souls were fed on the bread that cometh down from heaven. . . . The Lord came very near and convicted souls of their great need of his grace and love. We felt the necessity of presenting Christ as a Saviour who was not afar off, but nigh at hand.[3]

The students were overjoyed. It was as though they had turned a corner and come unexpectedly face to face with Jesus Himself, and He smiled at them. The experience expressed in Isaac Watts' hymn came alive for these youth:

> Forbid it Lord, that I should boast
> Save in the death of Christ my God;
> All the vain things that charm me most,
> I sacrifice them to His blood.

We have been told that "of all professing Christians Seventh-day Adventists should be foremost in uplifting Christ before the world."[4] The context of that oft-quoted remark was Ellen White's endorsement of this 1888 message, including the truth of the nature of Christ. Here are some samples of the 1888 messengers' heart burden to lift up Christ as a Savior "not afar off, but nigh at hand":

It has been Satan's work always to get men to think that God is as far away as possible. ... The great trouble with heathenism was to think that God was so far away.... Then the papacy came in, ... and again puts God and Christ so far away that nobody can come near to them. ... the false idea that He is so holy that it would be entirely unbecoming in Him to come near to us, and be possessed of such a nature as we have,—sinful, depraved, fallen human nature. Therefore Mary must be born immaculate ... and ... Christ must ... take His human nature in absolute sinlessness from her. ...

But if He comes no nearer to us than in a sinless nature, that is a long way off; because I need ... someone to help me who knows something about sinful nature; for that is the nature that I have; and such the Lord did take. He became one of us.[5]

You and I would give a great deal to be able to act as wisely as Jesus did. Every time he knew the right thing to say, and the right thing to do, and when not to say anything. Was there a person in the world who was as keen of intellect, who knew just how to meet every emergency as did Jesus. You know he was wiser than Solomon. How did he get that wisdom? ... How did it come to him?

(A voice) [someone in the congregation:] "It was intuition."

Then he was not like us at all. We read that "it behooved him to be made in all things like unto his brethren": that is, in every particular. We do not want to put the Lord off away from us, but he is one of us.... How did he come by his wisdom? ... He studied God's Word. ... He was wholly given to the Lord, knowing that there is no other use for man in this world but to serve the Lord.[6]

What Led These 1888 Messengers
To Present Jesus as "Nigh At Hand"?

They saw justification by faith itself in the light of the unique third angel's message of the cleansing of the sanctuary.[7] This gave them an insight that their contemporary Evangelicals could not have discovered. The clouds of many centuries that had partially hidden the Savior were rolled away. They rediscovered Paul's Romans 8 vision of Christ having been "sent in the likeness of sinful flesh, on account of sin: He condemned sin in the flesh."

After the apostle described his despair in Romans 7, he found joyful hope in the Good News of a Savior who came all the way to where we are. "There is therefore now no condemnation to those who are in Christ Jesus. … For the law of the Spirit of life in Christ Jesus has made me free from the law of sin and death."[8] How deep and thorough is Christ's deliverance from our long-entrenched compulsions to sin?

"No condemnation" means release from what the fallen Adam left to us—our inner sense of divine judgment which has hung over us all our lives.

Although these feelings of psychic wrong and maladjustment are deep and penetrating, "the law of the Spirit of life in Christ Jesus" goes even deeper and is more far-reaching. A new principle delivers from the fear, guilt, and moral disorder that have enslaved us, even from infancy.

No psychiatrist can accomplish such a catharsis of the human soul. This "law of the Spirit of life in Christ Jesus" heals. Wrongs and anxieties that even our parents could not relieve find inner cleansing. "When my father and my mother forsake me [where they must leave off], then the Lord will take me up."[9] Waggoner offers a breathtaking assurance: "He who takes God for the portion of his inheritance, has a power working in him for righteousness as much stronger than the power of inherited tendencies to evil, as our heavenly Father is greater than our earthly parents."[10]

Paul explains: "For what the law could not do in that it was weak through the flesh, God did by sending His own Son in the likeness of sinful flesh, on account of sin: He condemned sin in the flesh, that the righteous requirement of the law might be fulfilled in us who do not walk according to the flesh but according to the Spirit."[11]

The word "likeness" in the Greek means *identical, the same as*. It cannot mean *unlike or different from*. Christ who was (and remains) fully God now became (and remains) fully man as well. He built a divine-human bridge that spanned the gulf of alienation that sin has made. Its foundations reach all the way to the deepest root within the nature of the most helplessly lost sinner on earth.

Paul's intent was to present Christ as perfectly equipped to solve the problem of sinful alienation deep within our fallen nature. Here in our human flesh is the bastion where the dragon has made his last stand, and Christ confronts him there.

A fierce battle is being fought between Christ and Satan over this issue of whether that profound alienation can be resolved in "sinful flesh." There is no problem with sin being conquered in sinless nature different from ours. That battle was won long ago in heaven when two-thirds of the angels—in sinless nature—overcame Satan's temptations. That hasn't been an issue since. For Christ to come to earth to fight that same battle over again would be redundant.

The problem now is different. Sin has taken up residence in *fallen* human nature, in sinful flesh. Satan boasts, "You can't dislodge me from this lair! No human who has sinful flesh can overcome sin, for it is invincible! The human race belongs to me!"

He arrogantly claims that his invention of sin has developed to where it now proves God is wrong in the great controversy. Sin having taken root so deep in *fallen* human nature, it can only be tolerated and lightly "pardoned." God must either (a) continue to generously overlook it, or (b) in Roman Catholicism He must tackle the problem after death in a Purgatory when the sinner is shed of his sinful flesh. And most Christians implicitly agree with Satan in one or the other.

Now we are on the slimy trail of the "little horn" power. The bottom-line idea is that as long as you have a sinful nature, it is inevitable that you must continue sinning. Precisely Satan's point he has been contending for since his rebellion in heaven!

But Christ slew the dragon in his last lair, proved that human sin is willful and therefore unnecessary. And in mankind who believe, He created a new abhorrence of sin that leads to its final eradication. Thus He set the captive will of sinful man free to say "No" to sin, and through the faith *of* Jesus to become pure and holy.

When Peter foolishly tried to walk on the water and sank in the waves, he cried out, "Lord, save me."[12] We are all Peter sinking helplessly and we need that same Lifeguard "nigh at hand." We know only too well how strong is the undertow that sucks us into the maelstrom, and how dark are those depths.

Evil passions, hatreds, and lusts, lurk beneath the surface in all human hearts. Resentments, hatreds, and addictions that we seem powerless to control roll over us like ocean waves. Appetites, drugs, tobacco, alcohol, illicit loves, mock us as unconquerable. Deep emotions that the commandment forbids, like when it says "Thou shalt not covet thy neighbour's wife," are the same urges that caused Saul of Tarsus to recognize there was discreet adultery buried in his own naturally sinful heart. That's when he first understood how broad is the law of God, and also when he began to see the gospel as the only solution to his deep-seated problem.[13] He saw how to say "No!" to his sinful nature and to say "Yes!" to the Holy Spirit.

Youth (and many adults) with raging hormones despair of problems with illicit sex. The devil rejoices to boast that Christianity hasn't helped much, and the Islamic world in particular consider this as evidence of moral depravity built-in to Christianity. A survey of 1,006 American girls concludes: Religion-conscious girls are 86 percent more likely to say it's important to be a virgin at marriage than non-religion-conscious girls. However, *religion-conscious girls are only 14 percent more likely to be virgins than the non-religion-conscious girls."*[14]

Year after year about a million American teenage girls become pregnant. Not too long ago *Time* said that if present trends continue, 40 percent of today's 14-year-olds will be pregnant at least twice before their age 20.[15] According to polls, about 70 percent of American teens are into fornication, in violation (of course) of God's law of love. "If you tell that 70 percent to just say no, they laugh. And if they try to say no, they find it very difficult," says common wisdom. Such lack of self-control before marriage often programs these youth to future marital infidelity.

Meanwhile 17 million African young people have only mirrored Western mores and have died of AIDS, due largely to "sexual promiscuity" according to George F. Will in *Newsweek*.[16]

This is the world we live in. Multitudes suffer in despair, as Paul once did, for they don't want to slide down into moral darkness. They don't know how to handle temptation, peer pressure, hormonal urgings. Paul touched everyone's raw nerve when he complained of himself, "I do not understand what I do; for I don't do what I would like to do, but instead I do what I hate….Even though the desire to do good is in me, I am not able to do it. I don't do the good I want to do; instead, I do the evil that I do not want to do.… Evil is the only choice I have.… Sin … is at work in my body. What an unhappy man I am! Who will rescue me from this body that is taking me to death?"[17]

Whether this is the converted or unconverted Paul seems beside the point. He uses the corporate *ego,* referring to humanity in general "in Adam." Here is universal mankind crying, "Help! Help!"

And Help Is Much Closer Than We Adventists Have Thought

Paul answers his despairing question himself. He tells of a Savior who has come *very near.* But the problem is that the scandal of nearly two thousand years of so-called Christianity has removed that Savior. If it were not for this false doctrine that has put Him far away, it would be impossible for Christian youth, Seventh-day Adventists, to say, "I have a lot of work to do if I want to be saved," or "I wish I could be completely good, but it's not always easy," or "I want to serve God, but I find it very hard" (see statements cited in chapter two).

A Gallup poll found that an upsurge in America's religious interest has been canceled with a similar swing toward immoral behavior. "There is no doubt that religion is growing," Gallup reported. "But we find that there is very little difference in ethical behavior between church-goers and those who are not active religiously.… Levels of lying, cheating, and stealing are remarkably similar in both groups."[18] Not only is sexual morality in jeopardy, but basic honesty is dwindling also. An experiment reported in the March 2001 *Reader's Digest* uncovers the embarrassing fact that some "Christian" people were as willing to keep a "lost" billfold with $50 in it as non-Christians. How does the Savior feel about such news? Is it not embarrassing to Him?

Can't you hear Satan's hosts cheering at such news? When Jesus made His debut into the world, the angelic fanfare announced, "He will save His people *from* their sins."[19] What has happened? Why doesn't the world get to see more clear evidence that His people are indeed saved *from sin,* not *in* it?

The reason is that "the little horn" power has "cast truth down to the ground" and developed a "transgression of desolation."[20] It has hidden Christ from clear view while professing to worship Him, and has substituted a far-away "Christ" who cannot save *from* sin. And billions do not know the switch that has happened.

The 1888 message is unique in that it rediscovered both the closeness of the Savior, and how powerfully He can deliver *from* the tentacles of deep sin.

The Reason Why Christ Can Save Every Sinner On Earth

The 1888 message turns the spotlight on the book of Hebrews. Christ's closeness qualifies Him to penetrate to these inner recesses of our psychic, sinful alienation:

We see Jesus, who was made a little lower than the angels … that He, by the grace of God, might taste death for everyone. For it was fitting for Him … to make the author of their salvation perfect through sufferings.

For both He who sanctifies, and those who are being sanctified are all of one, for which reason He is not ashamed to call them brethren, saying … "I will put My trust in Him." …

Inasmuch then as the children have partaken of flesh and blood, He Himself likewise shared in the same, that through death He might destroy him who had the power of death, that is, the devil, and release those who through fear of death were all their lifetime subject to bondage. For indeed He does not give aid to angels, but He does give aid to the seed of Abraham [He took on Him the seed of Abraham, KJV].

Therefore, in all things He had to be made like His brethren, that He might be a merciful and faithful High Priest in things pertaining to God, to make propitiation for the sins of the people. For in that He Himself has suffered, being tempted, He is able to aid those who are tempted.[21]

A Unique Insight Comes Into Its Own on This Day of Atonement

(1) Although nobody else in history has done so, Christ has tasted our second death, the ultimate collective horror of all deepest despairs.

(2) He was "made perfect" through His sufferings.

(3) He is "one" with us.

(4) He calls us "brethren," that is, He is closer to us than family members to one another.

(5) Although He was always God in human flesh, He laid aside *the advantages* of His divinity so that as a child and then as a man He had to learn to "trust" in God.

(6) He "took part" of the "flesh and blood" of the *descendants of fallen Adam,* not that of the sinless Adam. That "flesh and blood" included the appetites and hormones of our "flesh and blood" we have today. These He said "No!" to.

(7) Specifically, He did not take the nature of sinless beings, but that of the "seed," the genetic *descendants of Abraham.* Thus, in the strongest language possible we are assured that Christ "took upon His sinless nature our sinful nature, *that He might know how to succor those that are tempted.*"[22]

(8) With no exception, He was "made like" unto us, the only exception being actual participation in sin.

(9) Thus He has become a "merciful and faithful High Priest," our divine-human Physician and Psychiatrist of our souls.

(10) In every way that we are tempted, He is able to save us from the sin itself.

Was He Tempted Only as the Sinless Adam Was Tempted?

Or was He tempted as we, the sinful *descendants* of Adam? Hebrews reiterates the answer: "We do not have a High Priest who cannot sympathize with *our* weaknesses, but was in all points tempted as *we* are, yet without sin."[23]

No matter how deep or how strong our temptation may be, Christ was tempted that same way, "yet without sin." And that's not all! A powerful "therefore" follows verse 15: "Let us therefore come boldly … and find grace to help in time of need." His "likeness of sinful flesh" gave Him perfect entrance to condemn that very sin—judge it, pronounce sentence on it, kill it. Be "bold" in Him; you deserve to receive the victory. Don't hang back timidly as though you are doomed to defeat. Step out and believe.

The Strange Opposition to the Nearness of the Savior

There are wonderful, highly respected people who tell us, no, this cannot be. Christ could not have been tempted as we are, for there were no TVs in His day, no 31 Flavors, no vodka, no Masseratis, etc. But that idea fails to appreciate what the Bible says. Every temptation to sin that we can experience is directed at our primal love of self; and Christ knows every avenue of that appeal. Knowing how strong the temptation is, He sympathizes with us, but even that is not all. Mere sympathy and pity would not help. You can sympathize with your injured dog and pity him. But Christ "succors" us. His full-time job is *saving* us from *yielding* to temptation. We "come boldly," not timidly, in a prayer of faith to "obtain" that help.

Note the clear insistence that although Christ came close to us, taking our sinful nature, He was "yet without sin." Not even by a thought would He *yield* to the tempter. "The prince of this world cometh, and hath nothing in me," He said.[24] He always remained "that holy One."[25] The struggle against sinful temptation was so fierce and so dangerous that He sweat drops of blood in His agony.[26]

That was a more terrible ordeal than any of us have known.

The struggle to yield our will to be "crucified with Him" may seem painful, but it is easier than our being crucified alone. Don't forget that Savior "nigh at hand." And living the life of resultant resurrection "with Him" is surely easier than wearing oneself out continuing to fight *against* the Holy Spirit.

A Promise Especially for These Last Days

"To him who overcomes I will grant to sit with Me on My throne, as I also overcame and sat down with My Father on His throne."[27] Now when sin and temptation seem stronger and more alluring than ever, when we are still weaker and more susceptible to falling, here comes this assurance that He gives the strength to overcome. But not on our own; *"even as I also overcame"* is the way.

This means that in these last days Christ's taking our fallen, sinful flesh becomes "a most precious" truth, more so than ever before. His overcoming is not only an example (an example is useless if you can't follow it!). But He becomes our Training-Exemplar. He identifies with you, and you identify with Him. Your temptation becomes His temptation; your success His victory, and your failure is His problem to solve. You are joined in a yoke with Him, and He does the pulling of the heavy weight. Your job is to stay with Him and to cooperate with Him, to "let" Him.[28]

Christ knew that in these last days Satan would lead multitudes into drug addiction, alcoholism, crime, lust, child abuse, homosexuality, pornography, fornication, adultery, bulimia, and countless temptations that seem irresistible because we share this common sinful nature. The lost sheep has strayed further from the fold than ever before, but the Good Shepherd goes further than ever before "until He find it." This means that as a divine Psychiatrist He probes ever more deeply into the why of our last-day weaknesses, and provides full healing. Sin abounding calls for grace *much more* abounding. And it is "nigh at hand."

Holiness Vis-à-vis Righteousness

Frequently Ellen White referred to the 1888 message as "the message of Christ's righteousness."[29] This significant phrase implicitly requires that in His incarnation Christ took the fallen, sinful nature of man. The reason is obvious.

"Righteousness" is a word that is never used of created beings with a sinless nature. We read of "holy angels" or "unfallen angels," but never do we find the phrase *righteous* angels. We read of Adam and Eve before the fall that they were "innocent and holy,"[30] but never do we see that they were *righteous*. They could have *developed* a "righteous character" if they had resisted temptation, but righteousness is always a term that means *holiness that has confronted temptation in sinful nature and has overcome.*

The word itself means justification, and something that is sinless cannot need justification. The innate meaning of the word is declaring something that has been crooked to be straightened.

"Righteous" therefore would be a misnomer for one who has only a sinless nature. *Such a being would be holy, but cannot be said to be righteous.* Christ was sinless, but He took our sinful, crooked nature and in it lived a perfect life of holiness. He fought and conquered the enemy in that flesh. *This is His righteousness.* And because the Father and the Son were always One, and the Father entered into the Son's battle on earth, Jesus could address Him both as "Holy Father" and as "Righteous Father."

If Christ had taken only the sinless nature of Adam before the fall, Inspiration would have to refer to the 1888 message of Christ's holiness, not "the message of Christ's righteousness." The fact that He perfectly "condemned sin in the flesh" of all fallen mankind gives Him title to that glorious name, "Christ *our* righteousness."

He will be successful in rescuing those who are sinking in these last-days' billows. Jude says He "is able to keep you from stumbling, and to present you faultless before the presence of His glory with exceeding joy." Revelation corroborates this promise by displaying a people who stand "without fault before the throne of God." At this time it must be said of His people, "The marriage of the Lamb has come, and His wife has made herself ready."[31]

The secret of their overcoming is not a special works program of trying harder than ever before; it is the recovery of a purer *faith* than any former generation have been able to grasp. The 1888 message is prophetically declared to be the "beginning" of the recovery of that faith.

The essence of that faith is a previously unrealized intimacy of sympathy with Christ, a heart-appreciation of Him, a "surveying" of His cross with the melting of frozen hearts. Nothing else but that non-egocentric, contrite concern for the honor of Him can "keep you from falling." As motives, selfish concern, fear of hell, hope of reward in heaven, will fail at last.

The Third Angel's Message and the Cleansing of the Sanctuary

Our addiction to sin stems from a sense of alienation from God and from one another with its profound loneliness. How has Christ abolished this darkness?

Those who were "aliens, … having no hope and without God in the world … have been made near by the blood of Christ." He has "abolished in His flesh the enmity, … that He might reconcile them … to God … through the cross, thereby putting to death the enmity."[32]

Even within the church, it's possible to go on Sabbath after Sabbath "having no hope, and without God in the world." But this alienation was endured by the tempted Jesus as He hung on His cross in His last hours. No one has ever felt so bereft of hope and joy as He when He cried out, "My God, My God, why have You forsaken Me?"

In that final hour of total darkness of soul, Jesus drank our bitter cup to its dregs. That's when He tasted real "death for every man." Do you feel as though the heavens are brass above you, the earth as iron beneath, that no one cares, that nothing lies before you but darkness, that Heaven seems to have slammed the door against you? *That is precisely how Jesus felt,* for that is a taste of the essence of "the second death." He endured it so that you might not have to feel that way.

Appreciate His Closeness to You

In His closing ministry on this great Day of Atonement He is working night and day to complete that reconciliation in the hearts of all who by faith sympathize with Him in that special work.

We can find the most intimate portrayals of His humiliation and excruciating personal pain and victory in what seems an unlikely place—the Psalms of David. At the 1895 General Conference Session Jones gave a series of studies on Christ as portrayed there.

Christ was in the place, and he had the nature, of the whole human race. And in him meet all the weaknesses of mankind, so that every man on the earth who can be tempted at all, finds in Jesus Christ power against that temptation. For every soul there is in Jesus Christ victory against all temptation, and relief from the power of it.[33]

On page 300 he discusses the fortieth psalm, showing how it is a self-written diary of Christ:

"Mine iniquities have taken hold upon me, so that I am not able to look up; they are more in number than the hairs of mine head: therefore my heart faileth me."

Who?—Christ. Where did he get iniquity?—Oh, "the Lord hath laid upon him the iniquity of us all."

Were they not more than the hairs of his head? ... Oh, "my heart faileth me," because of the enormity of the guilt and the condemnation of the sin—our sins that were laid upon him. Now return to the first verse of the fortieth psalm:—"I waited patiently for the Lord; and he inclined unto me, and heard my cry." Who?— Christ; and he was ourselves. Shall we, then, say the word: *I* waited patiently for the Lord; and he inclined unto *me,* and heard *my* cry?"—Assuredly. What, laden with sin as I am?—sinner as I am?— sinful flesh as I have?—How do I know that he hears my cry?— Ah, he has demonstrated it for a whole lifetime in my nearest of kin. He has demonstrated it in my flesh that he inclines,—leans over,—to listen to my cry. O, there are times, you know, when our sins seem to be so mountain-high. We are so discouraged by them. And Satan is right there ready to say, "Yes, you ought to be discouraged by them; there is no use of your praying to the Lord; he will not have anything to do with such as you are; you are too bad." ... Away with such thoughts! Not only will he hear, but ... the Lord is listening to hear the prayers of people laden with sin.

In that dark hour when He suffered alone, He built a bridge over the chasm of human alienation that sin has caused. His magnificent achievement is called "the atonement," the making at-one of those who were separated—we and God.

That alienation is the fundamental reason why so many youth seek illicit physical intimacies, now more than ever before. Their souls are hungry and empty for the reality which at-one-ment with Christ alone can fill.

They naturally imagine they will satisfy their soul-hunger by physical sexual intimacies. Frightening them with warnings of pregnancy, VD, AIDS, abortion, or hell, does nothing to help them resist temptation, for its roots run too deep. With AIDS becoming rampant, the world is at last realizing that sin is suicide. But fear of hell pathetically remains powerless to save from it.

Hope of reward is equally ineffective, hence the large percentage of "religion-conscious" girls and boys who are captive to temptation. This is the main reason why the Gallup poll is forced to record so little difference in moral and ethical behavior between Christians and non-Christians.

Abounding sin needs much more abounding grace—a revelation of the closeness of the Savior, an awareness that passes through the mind and penetrates to the heart. Only those who have received the atonement can be successful in ministering that grace to youth. The message of Christ's righteousness must at last come into its own to meet the need.

The Practical Value of Truth

Many are asking, How can I get close to Him? The answer may be clearer than we have thought. *It must be to believe how close He has come to you!*

Then the next step follows naturally: the honest heart *identifies with Him.* Paul said (according to the original language) that self is "crucified with Christ."[34] That is, his selfish pride, his perverse will that was contrary to the truth of God, his prideful ambition, his glorying in his own achievements or abilities or personality—this is his *ego:*

> When I survey the wondrous cross,
> On which the Prince of glory died,
> My richest gain I count but loss,
> And pour contempt on all my pride.

This does not mean that the one who believes in Christ grovels ever after in the dust of self-depreciation. One's sense of self-respect is never shattered, but enhanced. To be "crucified with Christ" means also to be resurrected with Him; "it is no longer I who live, but Christ lives in me." Now one finds his truest self-respect: "He pulled me out of a dangerous pit, out of the deadly quicksand. He set me safely on a rock and made me secure" (Psalm 4:2 TEV).

Believe that and you're forever riding high.

And side by side with an enhanced sense of self-respect comes a healthy repudiation of all "holier-than-thou" feelings. The closer one comes to Christ, the more sinful and unworthy one feels himself to be, but it's side by side with a deeper appreciation of what the Savior has done. We are never to judge ourselves, or give ourselves grade-points, nor can we claim to be sinless, for "if we say that we have no sin, we deceive ourselves, and the truth is not in us."

It is only when we continually "confess our sins, [that] he is faithful and just to forgive us our sins, and to cleanse us from all unrighteousness."[35] The proud and arrogant heresy of perfectionism can never rear its ugly head where the truth of Christ's righteousness is appreciated, for the song of every heart will be to give glory alone to Him.

Chapter Eight Endnotes

1 This is the basic thesis of A. T. Jones's *The Consecrated Way to Christian Perfection.*
2 Revelation 3:21.
3 *Review and Herald,* March 5, 1889.
4 *Gospel Workers,* p. 156.
5 Jones, *General Conference Bulletin,* 1895, p. 311.
6 E. J. Waggoner, *General Conference Bulletin,* 1897, p. 266.
7 "The third angel … pointed to the heavenly sanctuary, … to the most holy place, where Jesus stands before the ark, making His final intercession" (*Early Writings,* p. 254).
8 Romans 8:1, 2.
9 Psalm 27:10.
10 Waggoner, *The Everlasting Covenant,* p. 66, 67
11 Romans 8:3, 4.
12 Matthew 14:30.
13 Romans 7:7-11. It's vain to argue about who this passage refers to, the converted or the pre-converted Paul. We always have self to deny. Fallen nature will not be eradicated until glorification.
14 Leslie Jane Nonkin, *I Wish My Parents Understood,* NY, Penguin; emphasis supplied.
15 December 9, 1985.
16 January 10, 2000.
17 Romans 7:15-24, TEV.
18 Quoted in *Passing on the Torch,* by Roger Dudley (Review and Herald, 1986), p. 39
19 Matthew 1:21.
20 Daniel 8:12, 13.
21 Hebrews 2:9-11, 14-18.
22 *Medical Ministry,* p. 181, emphasis added.
23 Hebrews 4:14, 15.
24 John 14:30, KJV.
25 Luke 1:35.
26 Hebrews 5:7; 12:3, 4.
27 Revelation 3:21.
28 Matthew 11:28-30.
29 MS 15, 1888; *Through Crisis to Victory,* p. 294; MS 24, 1888; *Selected Messages,* Book Three, pp. 168-172; *Review and Herald,* July 23, 1889, May 27, *Extra,* December 23, 1890.
30 *Patriarchs and Prophets,* p. 48; *Seventh-day Adventist Bible Commentary,* Vol. 1, p. 1083.
31 Jude 24; Revelation 12:17; 14:5, 12; 19:7, 8.
32 Ephesians 2:12-16.
33 1895 *General Conference Bulletin,* p. 254. Cf. Psalm 22:1-24; 69:7-21; Isaiah 53:4-6.
34 Galatians 2:20.
35 1 John 1:8, 9.

THE NEW COVENANT BREAKS THROUGH THE FOG

It's a pity when a fresh revelation of truth excites opposition among God's people. And it's doubly so when that newly revealed truth is especially "sent" by the Lord for a good reason.

The Good News of the new covenant was an essential part of the 1888 message, but it aroused controversy with years of resistance. Galatians says that the confusion of old covenant ideas "gives birth to bondage."[1] Investigation reveals that for years an infiltration of those ideas held the ascendancy among us, yet we seem unaware of the reality. Such widespread "bondage" is one reason why we lose so many of our youth when they come to thinking for themselves.

Ellen White several times says that she was "shown" by the Lord that the 1888 view is the true one, and that the brethren who opposed it were wasting their time.[2] She considered it not only to be authentic biblically, but beautiful in its clarity and motivating power.

In 1738 John Wesley chanced on a meeting where someone was reading what Luther wrote about justification by faith. "I did feel my heart strangely warmed," he recalled. Many who have had the privilege of reading the Jones-Waggoner presentations of the two covenants testify the same. The Holy Spirit gave the two young men a brilliant insight into "most precious" truth.

As a newly baptized Seventh-day Adventist teen I went through four years of public high school almost alone in my faith. The Sabbath was a never-ending problem. I heard, "You're a Jew!" "You're under the law!" "You ought to read Galatians, that'll straighten you out." I tried to read Galatians, but it confused me. On the surface it appeared to support my ridiculing friends, but I knew the Sabbath truth somehow had to be right.

I went to Sabbath school and church every week, even to camp meetings. Then for the first time I entered a Seventh-day Adventist school, a college. Even then no one helped me understand Galatians.

Finally in my senior college year I chanced to discover E. J. Waggoner's long out-of-print *The Glad Tidings* with its two chapters on the covenants. Never had I seen such Good News in the gospel! It made sense. Only much later did I learn what Ellen White had said about his view. Nevertheless, on the spot I accepted it from Waggoner, knowing nothing of who he was or of the 1888 history. The truth "strangely warmed my heart" as Luther's had warmed Wesley's. I grabbed it. (My conscience had forced me to accept the Sabbath truth on my own nine years earlier when my Presbyterian pastor had tried to dissuade me.)

In this chapter we want to let the Bible unfold this precious message as Waggoner saw it. May your heart also be "strangely warmed."

The New Covenant Is God's One-sided Promise

Long before the "old covenant" came into being the Lord originally made the "everlasting covenant"—God's promise to make His people "complete in every good work to do His will … through Jesus Christ."[3]

That is a big project, because all mankind have not only sinned but have fallen into a slavery to sin and *ego*-centeredness so deep that the roots seem bottomless. The new covenant is the news of how God solves this problem and provides full healing.

There is no need to be confused by artificial definitions. Theologians talk about the "Adamic covenant," "the Noachian covenant," and the "Abrahamic covenant," but these are all the same "new" or "everlasting covenant" that God promised, only under different circumstances. The principle and the promise were always the same—the new covenant is God's *unilateral* promise to us.

And that's just the problem why this 1888 truth has been so opposed—fear of the Good News being too good.

This covenant (or promise) was made more distinct and far reaching in the Lord's conversations with Abraham. He virtually promised the old man the sky! In him "all the families of the earth shall be blessed." The promise included land "northward, southward, eastward, and westward.""Count the stars if you are able to number them," God said."So shall your descendants be."

Staggering! The promises include:

(1) Abraham's descendants will become the greatest nation in the world;

(2) The Messiah will come through them;

(3) In them every family in the world will be "blessed;"

(4) The land of Canaan will be their possession;

(5) Even more, the promise includes the whole world, which must be the new earth;[4]

(6) Since the earth is to be an "everlasting possession," the "new covenant" must include everlasting life as well in the earth made new;[5]

(7) Moreover, since only righteousness can dwell in this new earth,[6] the new covenant promise includes making righteous all who believe;

(8) The down-payment on all this incredible blessing would be a miraculous birth;[7] an "impossible" conception will take place enabling Abraham's aged and sterile wife Sarah to bear a son whose name would be Isaac ("laughter");

(9) The world's Savior is not to come through Ishmael, who is a symbol of a do-it-yourself works program, but

(10) Christ will come through Isaac "the child of promise." This will forever demonstrate that Abraham's true descendants are those only who have his faith.

What Promises Did God Ask Abraham To Make In Return?

If you read carefully, you will see that the answer is—none! The new covenant promise is entirely one-sided. God does all the promising. He does not ask us to make promises to Him, for He knows we cannot keep them.

But was Abraham expected to do nothing? What was his part in the bargain? The answer is an astounding one, that many have trouble with: only one thing, *believe*. "He believed in the Lord, and He accounted it to him for righteousness."[8]

Difficult as it may be to confess, we must recognize that all the Lord asked from Abraham was *faith*. This does not mean that He did not *expect* obedience or that good works were not important. The Lord was teaching Abraham the principle of righteousness by faith. Once Abraham learned to *believe,* true obedience would follow as surely as fruit follows the blossom. And it did, for the Lord said later, "I have known him … to do righteousness and justice."[9]

The ancient Israelites misunderstood the covenant, but Paul got to the heart of it. Circumcision became for them the symbol of their do-it-yourself, works-and-obedience program. Paul's point is neat: Abraham's faith "was counted unto him for righteousness" *before,* not *after,* he was circumcised.[10] Brilliant insight! This is how the apostle proved that justification is by faith alone. Six times in Romans 4 we read that Abraham is *"our* father," the spiritual ancestor of all who exercise faith.

But Paul is not putting down obedience, for the word "righteousness" includes true justification, which word implies straightening out what was crooked. It is being put right, that is, learning genuine obedience through receiving the atonement. It becomes possible only through faith, but the Good News is that it is not only possible but certain, *if like Abraham we will believe God's magnificent promise.*

God's Covenant Is Always His One-sided Promise

The 1888 messengers saw a beautiful garden of truth where others saw only a barren desert:

The covenant and promise of God are one and the same.… God's covenants with men can be nothing else than promises to them.…

After the Flood God made a "covenant" with every beast of the earth, and with every fowl; but the beasts and the birds did not promise anything in return. Genesis 9:9-16. They simply received the favor at the hand of God. That is all we can do—receive. God promises us everything that we need, and more than we can ask or think, as a gift. We give Him ourselves, that is, nothing. And He gives us Himself, that is, everything. That which makes all the trouble is that even when men are willing to recognize the Lord at all they want to make bargains with Him. They want it to be an equal, "mutual" affair—a transaction in which they can consider themselves on a par with God. ...

The gospel was as full and complete in the days of Abraham as it has ever been or ever will be. No addition to it or change in its provisions or conditions could possibly be made after God's oath to Abraham. Nothing can be taken away from it as it thus existed, and not one thing can ever be required from any man more than what was required of Abraham.[11]

What could be more difficult than making dead people come alive? But that's what the One specializes in who promises us the new covenant. He "gives life to the dead and calls those things which do not exist as though they did."[12] In other words, He already counts blessings as reality that you have not yet even begun to see. When we learn to believe, we too will "call those things which do not exist as though they did," because the Word of God declares that these apparently impossible blessings *will be.*

How the World's Best People Invented the Old Covenant

Four hundred and thirty years went by. When the Lord brought Abraham's descendants out of Egyptian slavery, He wanted to impress on their minds the same "new" covenant He had made long before with their father Abraham:

You have seen what I did to the Egyptians, and how I bore you on eagles' wings and brought you to Myself. Now therefore, if you will indeed obey My voice and keep [Heb., *shamar,* cherish, preserve; see Genesis 2:15] My covenant, then you shall be a special treasure to Me above all people for all the earth is Mine. And you shall be to Me a kingdom of priests and a holy nation.[13]

The Hebrew word for "obey" means primarily to "listen."[14] Any parent knows that obedience is easier if the child will but listen. Since

God's covenant is always His promise, to "keep My covenant" means to cherish and to appreciate the promise He made to their forefather, Abraham.

In other words, if Israel at Sinai would *believe* as Abraham did, they would become a "kingdom of priests, and an holy nation," the greatest on earth. The whole world would beat a path to their door to learn about righteousness by faith which solves all human problems. "If they would simply keep God's covenant, keep the faith, and believe God's promise, they would be a 'peculiar treasure' unto God," says Waggoner.[15]

To "bear ... on eagles' wings" is the meaning of the Latin word from which we get our word "succor." We read in the KJV that Christ "is able to succour them that are tempted."[16] The deliverance from Egypt was designed to teach this same glorious new covenant truth—that the Lord saves us like a mother eagle saves her young. Israel did nothing to effect their deliverance from Egypt except to *let* the Lord do it for them, as a baby eagle lets its mother "succor" it. But the people did not want the lesson. *They wanted a works program.* So do we!

Obsessed with legalism, unbelief blinded their souls so that they could not appreciate God's grace as Abraham did. Their response was not like his, to *believe* with a contrite heart. Instead, they solemnly promised to be good, that they would obey: "Then all the people answered together and said, 'All that the Lord has spoken we will do.'"[17] *This was the old covenant.* It was the promise of the people:

> These two covenants exist today. The two covenants are not matters of time, but of condition. Let no one flatter himself that he cannot be bound under the old covenant, thinking that its time has passed. The time for that is passed only in the sense that "the time past of our life may suffice us to have wrought the will of the Gentiles, when we walked in lasciviousness, lusts, excess of wine, revelings, banquetings, and abominable idolatries." 1 Peter 4:3, KJV.[18]

This promise of "all the people" was a detour occasioned by their unbelief. If the people would not keep step with Him, God must now humble Himself to keep step with them. He must ratify their old covenant with animal's blood and show them the futility of their self-confident legalism. Galatians says that the "law … was added because of transgressions."[19] The word "added" means "emphasized," "underlined," or "articulated." Waggoner makes this passage clear:

> The law was given to show them [Israel] that they had not faith and so were not true children of Abraham, and were therefore in a fair way to lose the inheritance. God would have put His law into their hearts even as He put it into Abraham's heart, if they had believed. But when they disbelieved, yet still professed to be heirs of the promise, it was necessary to show them in the most marked manner that their unbelief was sin…. They had the same spirit as their descendants, who asked, "What must we *do,* to be doing the work of God?" John 6:28. … Unless they saw their sin, they could not avail themselves of the promise. Hence the necessity of the speaking of the law.[20]

Now must come the terrors of Mt. Sinai, which were completely unnecessary for Abraham with his heart-faith. Since the people had now instituted the old covenant by making their arrogant promise, the Lord is obliged to communicate His law to them through this second-choice method.[21]

God did not need to frighten Abraham with "thunders and lightnings" and earthquakes, for He wrote His holy law in his humble believing heart. The old covenant depends on fear as its motivation to produce "the works of the law," because the motivation of faith has not yet been realized.

For example, to refrain from illicit sex because of fear of AIDS or shame is old covenant legalism. To keep the Sabbath because of fear of being lost is also legalism. It is good to refrain from illicit sex, and it is good to keep the Sabbath, but the motive that is truly effective is supplied only by the grace of God in the new covenant.

The new covenant is heart-religion, an inexpressible gratitude and awe imposed by grace. The Lord promises, "I will put My laws in their mind and write them on their hearts."[22] This means more than memorizing certain phrases. It means a love affair with grace and truth.

How does the Lord write His law in human hearts? It's easy to give a glib answer, "By the Holy Spirit." But *how* does He do it? By capturing the affections of the soul, which Ellen White often said is "heart work."

The alienated heart is reconciled to God through that "blood of the cross." When "the love of Christ constrains us," we become new creatures.[23] The cold, stony heart we were born with becomes melted; a new spirit fills the heart. We learn to hate the sins we once loved, and we love harmony and reconciliation with the Savior. In short it is heart-appreciation of the love that led Him to the cross.

Under the new covenant, the ten commandments become ten great promises. For example, says the Lord, when you *believe* that "I am the Lord your God, who brought you out of the land of Egypt, out of the house of bondage," inexpressible gratitude motivates you. Then "you will never fall into adultery," or "murder," or "steal," or fall into any other sin. An appreciation of that cross cleanses those buried motivations of sin and selfishness that have such deep roots.

The fruit is not the cold "works of the law" that are motivated by fear, but a selfless devotion to Christ which alone is true obedience. *"Agape* is the fulfilling of the law."[24]

> God's precepts are promises; they *must* necessarily be such, because He knows that we have no power. All that God requires is what He *gives*. When He says, "Thou shalt not," we may take it as His assurance that if we but believe Him He will preserve us from the sin against which He warns us.[25]

The Common but Terrible Bondage of the Old Covenant

Making old covenant promises to God "gives birth to bondage," says Galatians. It's a terrible thing to drag unsuspecting young Christians into this spiritual "bondage." But this is what happens when we lead them to make these vain promises to God.

For example, children and youth are led to promise to keep the ten commandments "every day," and never to go where those commandments tell them "nay." Soon they forget or are enticed into a mistake. They forget to keep their solemn promise, and their failures make them feel alienated from the grace of God. They often abandon hope of salvation. Some few find their way back from the bondage of the old covenant into the liberty of the new, but many others fall and never rise again.

It is not only useless but harmful to lead children to make promises to God to be obedient forever. *Not that it is wrong to obey;* the problem is that the old covenant is not *the way* to obey. For example, it is well known that it is useless to lead a cigarette addict to *promise* never to smoke again, or an alcoholic to *promise* never to drink again.

If there are still lethal injections of old covenant teaching in our literature for children and youth, the "bondage" thus ministered is one reason why so many become discouraged. Many sincerely unaware teach the same view of the covenants as those who rejected the 1888 message a century ago, that God's covenant was His "contract" with the people.

Here is the root reason why the "contract" idea of the covenant leads into spiritual bondage:

> You are weak in moral power, in slavery to doubt, and controlled by the habits of your life of sin. Your promises and resolutions are like ropes of sand. You cannot control your thoughts, your impulses, your affections. The knowledge of your broken promises and forfeited pledges weakens your confidence in your own sincerity, and causes you to feel that God cannot accept you [this is what Paul means when he says that the old covenant "gives birth to bondage"]. ... What you need to understand is the true force of the will. ... Everything depends on the right action of the will. ... You cannot change your heart, you cannot of yourself give to God its affections; but you can *choose* to serve him. ... Thus your whole nature will be brought under the control of the Spirit of Christ; your affections will be centered upon Him, your thoughts will be in harmony with Him.[26]

Even some of our beloved hymns are permeated with old covenant concepts that "give birth to bondage." The effect is subliminal. Sincere Christians who are bound in depression unconsciously assimilate respected hymns or "gospel" songs that convey "under the law" or *ego*-oriented messages. They listen to "Christian" radio stations all day and wonder why they are still depressed.

A Hidden Source of Depression

Our Savior administers His new covenant promise through the ministry of the Holy Spirit, but any false doctrine hinders His work. The Pope of Rome claims to be the Vicar of Christ, His representative on earth, taking His place since Christ has ascended to heaven. If that were true, it would be bad news for everyone, for the Pope can do nothing to help you and me. He is too far away and too busy with too many people.

But Jesus said that His true Vicar on earth is the Holy Spirit. He constantly tries to lead us into the new covenant. This is Good News, because He "succors" us even more than Jesus could if He were here in person. In fact, He is called the Spirit of Christ, Christ's Representative, divested of physical limitations, but acting in His stead, encouraging us to believe His promise as Abraham did.

As Jesus is closer to us than popular teaching allows, so the Holy Spirit is closer to us than we have thought. He is as much a Friend as Jesus is. He is on our side, trying to get us ready to enter heaven. To this end, truth is important.

Jesus introduces the Holy Spirit by giving Him a special name— "another Helper."[27] He is "another *parakletos*," that is, a Replacement for Himself sent "in My name," says Jesus. The Greek word means "the one who is called to come and sit down beside you forever" (*para,* as in parallel—two railroad tracks are parallel, and they always stay together; and *kletos,* the One called). He will never leave us, although we have power to grieve Him and drive Him off if we choose.

We are closer to Christ today by the Spirit than the Twelve were 2000 years ago when they walked and talked with Him personally. He is also a Master Teacher and Stimulator of our memory, for Jesus said that "He will teach you all things, and bring to your remembrance all things that I said to you."[28]

The Holy Spirit's Specialty: Teaching the New Covenant

The Good News of the Holy Spirit's work in the new covenant shines brightly in the 1888 message:

It can never be repeated too often, that under the reign of grace it is just as easy to do right, as under the reign of sin it is easy to do wrong. This must be so; for if there is not more power in grace than there is in sin, then there can be no salvation from sin.... Let no one ever attempt to serve God with any thing but the present, living power of God, that makes him a new creature.... Then the service of God will indeed be in "newness of life;" then it will be found that his yoke is indeed "easy" and his burden "light;" then his service will be found indeed to be with "joy unspeakable and full of glory."[29]

As boundless grace is given to everyone bringing salvation to the extent of its own full measure, then if any one does not have boundless salvation, why is it?—Plainly it can be only because he will not take that which is given.[30]

It is not you who are to do that which he [the Lord] pleases: but, "It shall accomplish that which I please." You are not to read or hear the word of God, and say, I must do that, I will do that. You are to open the heart to that word, that it may accomplish the will of God in you. ... The word of God itself is to do it, and you are to let it. "Let the word of Christ dwell in you."[31]

Note how Ellen White agrees with this Good News message:

Do not ... conclude that the upward path is the hard and the downward road the easy way. All along the road that leads to death there are pains and penalties, there are sorrows and disappointments, there are warnings not to go on. God's love has made it hard for the heedless and headstrong to destroy themselves. ... All the way up the steep road leading to eternal life there are well-springs of joy to refresh the weary.[32]

The last page of the Bible extends the final invitation, "The Spirit and the bride say, Come."[33] He is appealing to people who we may think are hopeless, and the church which is to be the Bride of Christ is to be in perfect sympathy with Him in His concern for them. Many more than we suppose will respond to the new covenant gospel. God intended that its light should lighten the earth with glory in the 1888 era.

Today, God's true, honest people are still in symbolic "Babylon." They will take the place of those who will leave the remnant church. They have long professed the truth but rejected it in heart, and have resisted the kind of self-crucified-with-Christ devotion that the *agape* of Christ demands.

Meanwhile: the Holy Spirit Is Holding the Four Winds of Strife

Angels and the Holy Spirit still cooperate in holding back the final outburst of strife and plagues symbolized by the loosing of the "four winds."[34] You cannot safely drive down the highway unless God restrains some drunk or drug-crazed maniac from plowing into you. The entire world would be engulfed in ruin unless the Holy Spirit were restraining the evil about to burst loose.

But He is being withdrawn from the world, not because He wants to leave but because mankind are steadily driving Him off. "Today if you will hear His voice, do not harden your hearts."[35] The final sin against Him which is unpardonable is that last choice to reject His pleading when He says, "This is the way, walk in it."

In the meantime, the evidence is clear: the Holy Spirit is powerless to withhold human strife unless His people faithfully proclaim the sealing message, which is that "most precious" new covenant truth. The multiple wars and massacres of the past century cannot have been God's will for the world.

Only one thing seems truly difficult for us—to believe how good the Good News is. Our constant battle is to "fight the good fight of faith."[36] Mankind is so held captive in unbelief that nothing can break through those chains except the truth of the cross of Christ and the full reality of the Holy Spirit's constant ministry. He is still the Vicar of the great High Priest whose special work is cleansing the heavenly sanctuary. And the unique message associated with that work is what an inspired voice declared is "most precious."

Let's get in tune with it.

Chapter Nine Endnotes

[1] Galatians 4:24.

[2] "Since I made the statement last sabbath that the view of the covenants as it had been taught by Brother Waggoner was truth, it seems that great relief has come to many minds." "Night before last I was shown that evidences in regard to the covenants were clear and convincing. You … are spending your investigative powers for naught to produce a position on the covenants to vary from the position that Brother Waggoner has presented…the true light which shineth. … The covenant question is a clear question and would be received by every candid, unprejudiced mind" (Letters 30, 59, 1890, to Uriah Smith).

[3] Hebrews 13:20, Genesis 17:7; Revelation 13:8.

[4] Cf. Romans 4:13.

[5] John 3:16.

[6] 2 Peter 3:13.

[7] Genesis 12:1-3, 7; 13:14-17; 15:1-6, 18; 17:1-8, 21; 18:14; Romans 4:11.

[8] Genesis 15:6.

[9] Genesis 18:19.

[10] Romans 4:1-12.

[11] Waggoner, *The Glad Tidings,* pp. 71-73. Originally published 1900. The edition quoted here was authorized by the General Conference to be re-published by Pacific Press in 1971 after some panentheistic ideas that were never orignally part of the Waggoner message that slipped in, were edited out.

[12] Romans 4:13, 14, 16-18.

[13] Exodus 19:4-6.

[14] Hebrew *shamea,* translated in the Old Testament 760 times as hear, 196 times as hearken; 81 times as obey.

[15] Waggoner, *op. cit.,* p. 99.

[16] Hebrews 2:18.

[17] Exodus 19:8.

[18] Waggoner, *op. cit.,* p. 100.

[19] Galatians 3:19.

[20] Waggoner, *op. cit.,* p. 74.

[21] Exodus 19:16-18; 20:1-20.

[22] Cf. Hebrews 8:8-12.

[23] 2 Corinthians 5:14-16.

[24] Romans 13:10.

[25] Waggoner, *op. cit.,* p. 77; cf. Ellen White, *Commentary,* Vol. 1, p. 1105.

[26] *Steps to Christ,* p. 47.

[27] John 14:16-18, 26.

[28] John 14:26.

[29] Jones, *Review and Herald,* September 1, 1896.

[30] *Ibid.,* September 22, 1896.

[31] *Ibid.,* October 20, 1896.

[32] *Thoughts From the Mount of Blessing,* pp. 139, 140.

[33] Revelation 22:17.

[34] Revelation 7:1.

[35] Hebrews 3:7, 8.

[36] 1 Timothy 6:12.

Chapter Ten

THE STORY OF 1888: WHAT REALLY HAPPENED?

[*Note:* Statements quoted in this chapter can be verified in the four-volume set, *The Ellen G. White 1888 Materials.* Numbers in brackets refer to page numbers.]

What made the 1888 conference "epochal" and "crucial"? It was both the character of the special message presented, and its strange reception. On the one hand, the message was profoundly unique, the most clear since the Midnight Cry of 1844; on the other, its reception was phenomenal, the most emphatic and determined resistance ever known within the Advent Movement.

Must we understand the history? Or can we merely content ourselves with an idea of the message and forget its story? The answer is important.

History is always interwoven with God's message. Both the Old and New Testaments are historical documents laced with salvation truth. We cannot properly appreciate the *gospel* of Christ without understanding the *history* of His humble life and ministry, His crucifixion and resurrection. Neither can we appreciate the 1888 *message* without understanding the *history* that accompanied it. One important reason why so many value the message so little is that they have misunderstood its history.

The gospel story touches every one's raw nerve of conscience because we see ourselves in those who rejected the Savior. Thus we are led to true repentance, knowing that their sin is our sin but for the grace of God.

In the same way we see ourselves in our brethren at odds with the Lord Jesus Christ in the 1888 story. The import is "that no flesh should glory in His presence."[1] That of course is genuine justification by faith, for "it is the work of God in laying the glory of man in the dust, and doing for man that which it is not in his power to do for himself."[2] Understanding history is a part of it.

And knowing our 1888 history is a positive, upbeat experience. In God's work, the real truth is always *good* news. It provides hope for the future because it illuminates the mysteries of the past and reveals the present strategies of the great controversy between Christ and Satan. Corrie Ten Boom says, "Memories are the key not to the past, but to the future."[3]

We definitely lost a battle in our 1888 experience, but not the war. In order to win at last, we must understand how the battle was lost. We might well paraphrase George Santayana, "If the Seventh-day Adventist denomination does not know its history, it is fated to repeat it."[4]

In this present era of offshoots, heresies and weakened conviction, the full truth of 1888 establishes confidence in the ultimate triumph of the Seventh-day Adventist Church. When we correctly understand our past we shall be better prepared to understand the perplexing present and prepare for that perilous future.

The Story of What Happened

Very simply told, the main details are these:

(1) The Lord raised up two young men whom Ellen White said were His "delegated messengers," "whom God has commissioned," and gave them a clearer understanding of the gospel in the third angel's message than others had; then He sent them with this "most precious message" to the General Conference delegates gathered at Minneapolis in 1888.[5]

(2) A.T Jones and E.J. Waggoner presented a concept of Christ's righteousness which she later identified as the "beginning" of the loud cry of Revelation 18:1-4. And since the loud cry can't come until first the latter rain is received, it was also the beginning of that.[6]

(3) At Minneapolis and for a decade following, Ellen White endorsed their message over 370 times, using the most enthusiastic language she could find. Nothing in her long lifetime ever made her so happy. Unless we give due regard to her testimony, we may accept

counterfeit messages and cast ourselves adrift at sea without an anchor.

(4) The two delegates' manner of presenting their message was simple, clear, and even at times beautiful. She said they gave evidence that God gave them "heavenly credentials," and they conducted themselves in the face of opposition as "a Christian gentleman" should. She said they presented their message "with beauty and loveliness," and "with grace, and power."[7] This does not mean that they were perfect or that they made no mistakes; but the overwhelming impact of their presentations was on the positive side—Christlike, she often said.[8]

(5) According to her testimony, the great majority of the delegates reacted negatively to the message. Her eyewitness accounts say: "The spirit and influence of the ministers generally who have come to this meeting is to discard light."[9] "Our ministering brethren ... are here only to shut out the Spirit of God from the people."[10] "Opposition rather than investigation is the order of the day."[11] Two other eyewitnesses report:

> In 1888 I was sent as a delegate from the Kansas Conference to the General Conference held that year in Minneapolis, Minnesota, that notable conference long to be remembered by many. ... I am sorry for anyone who was at the Conference in Minneapolis in 1888 who does not recognize that there was opposition and rejection of the message that the Lord sent to His people at that time.[12]

> The writer of this tract, then a young man, was present at that [1888] conference meeting, and saw and heard many of the various things that were done and said in opposition to the message then presented. ... When Christ was lifted up as the only hope of the church and of all men, the speakers met a united opposition from nearly all the senior ministers. They tried to put a stop to this teaching by Elders Waggoner and Jones.[13]

Thirteen years later, a prominent speaker at the 1901 session reported:

There are many in this audience who can remember ... when, thirteen years ago at Minneapolis, God sent a message to his people. ... For the past thirteen years this light has been rejected and turned against by many, and they are rejecting it and turning from it today.[14]

A former General Conference president, not present at the 1888 conference but close to the issues, adds: "The message has never been received, nor proclaimed, nor given free course as it should have been in order to convey to the church the measureless blessings that were wrapped within it."[15]

A. W. Spalding reports, "There was personal pique at the messengers," and "a tumult of clerical passions was let loose."[16]

A speaker at the 1893 General Conference session openly declared that "the brethren in that fearful position in which they stood ... at Minneapolis ... rejected the latter rain—the loud cry—of the third angel's message."[17] Those present very well knew he was telling the truth; no one challenged him.

(6) A few other delegates, notably Ellen White, S. N. Haskell and Willie White, were favorable. The rejection was not total, but our "long journey" and spiritual famine of more than a century stem from this experience. Heaven was forced to withdraw for "many more years" the blessings of the latter rain and the loud cry.[18]

In spite of the fact that the two messengers spoke at camp meetings and General Conference sessions, constant leadership rejection nullified or at least neutralized their best efforts. The brethren's persistent attitude as late as 1896 kept the message "from our people, in a great measure," and "in a great degree ... from the world."[19] Ellen White explains how this process operated:

The very men who need this work ... have themselves barred the way that it shall not come. ... When the leaders get out of the way, the work will be progressive in Battle Creek. ... The position taken at Battle Creek has been the pulse-beating of many churches. ... The Lord God of Israel has opened the windows of heaven to send the earth rich floods of light, but in many cases there was no place made to receive it or give it room. ... [By]

ministers, pastors, and those who stand in responsible posi-
tions ... barriers have been thrown up, and the streams of
salvation turned aside into another channel.[20]

(7) What happened at Minneapolis was more serious than mere
human judgment could appreciate. The inspired prophet saw beneath
the surface: "The spirit which prevailed ... [which] was a controlling
power at that meeting ... was cruelty to the Spirit of God."[21] Three
years later she repeated this frightful statement, "I know that at the
time the Spirit of God was insulted."[22]

(8) Ellen White, Jones, and Waggoner held meetings during the
winter of 1888-1889 and even into 1890 where the Lord worked in an
unusual manner. The people were ready to accept the message gladly,
giving occasion for a superficial judgment prevalent today that claims
the message was warmly accepted in the end. But the influence of the
leaders at Battle Creek discouraged and hindered the confused but
favorable laity. She wrote burning messages of reproof, pleading for
the brethren to accept the message and stop hindering its impact on
the people.

She said in 1890, "For nearly two years we have been urging the
people to come up and accept the light and truth concerning the
righteousness of Christ, and they do not know whether to come and
take hold of this precious truth or not." Her article in the *Review and
Herald* of a week later told the reason:

> I have tried to present the message to you as I have understood
> it, but how long will those at the head of the work keep
> themselves aloof from the message of God? ... Our young men
> look to our older brethren, and ... they see that they do not accept
> the message, but treat it as though it were of no consequence.[23]

(9) So persistent was the opposition that Ellen White's support
upset the General Conference leadership. Robert W. Olson of the White
Estate declares that she was "publicly defied."[24] She herself said, "Elder
Butler presented the matter before me in a letter stating that my
attitude at that Conference [1888] just about broke the hearts of some
of our ministering brethren at that meeting."[25]

(10) So compelling was the evidence supporting the message that a number of brethren were virtually forced to confess that they had taken a wrong stand at and after Minneapolis. One after another asked for pardon, sometimes with tears. *Review* editor Uriah Smith and former General Conference president G. I. Butler had influenced many to reject the message and both in time confessed their wrong attitude.

However, these confessions could not undo the evil that the 1888 era rejection had caused. Their resistance of the latter rain and the loud cry, so far as that generation was concerned, was conclusive. The important factor is not the personal salvation of the erstwhile rejectors, but whether the loud cry of Revelation 18 was allowed to go *to the world*. "In a great degree" it wasn't.

Later on some of the most notable confessors returned to their previous stance of opposition, so that Ellen White was forced to say, "This blind warfare is continued. ... They have never seen clearly since [Minneapolis], and they never will."[26] In late 1892, after most of the "confessions" had come in, Ellen White said that "not one" of those who initially rejected the message ever recovered the blessing they had forfeited. History confirms her judgment:

> Who of those that acted a part in the meeting at Minneapolis have come to the light and received the rich treasures of truth which the Lord sent them from heaven? Who have kept step with the Leader, Jesus Christ? Who have made full confession of their mistaken zeal, their blindness, their jealousies and evil surmisings, their defiance of truth? Not one.[27]

(11) But on the surface, all appeared to be well in the 1890s. Reports of the progress of "the cause" appeared in the *Review* week by week as though nothing were wrong. But something *was* wrong. Speaking at the 1901 session regarding those dark years of the 1890s, Ellen White said:

> The brethren assented to the light given, but ... the light that was given was not acted upon. It was assented to but no special change was made to bring about such a condition of things that the power of God could be revealed among His people. Year after

year the same acknowledgement was made. … It is a marvel to me that we stand in as much prosperity as we do today.[28]

A little later she added, "Many … have been more or less out of line since the Minneapolis meeting."[29] She hoped they would come into line.

(12) Even the new General Conference president elected in 1888 failed to stand on the right side, and he lent his influence against the message. He supported it initially, but eight years after Minneapolis Ellen White felt forced to write the following about him:

> He is leading other minds to view matters in a perverted light. He has given unmistakable evidence that he does not regard the testimonies which the Lord has seen fit to give His people, as worthy of respect, or as of sufficient weight to influence his course of action.

> I am distressed beyond any words my pen can trace. Unmistakably Elder Olsen has acted as did Aaron, in regard to these men [A. R. Henry and Harmon Lindsay, General Conference leaders] who have been opposed to the work of God ever since the Minneapolis meeting.[30]

A few months earlier she had written him personally, "I have been shown that the people at large do not know that the heart of the work is being diseased and corrupted at Battle Creek."[31] In an 1897 letter she said, "The President of the General Conference … went directly contrary to the cautions and warnings given him" concerning the 1888 aftermath.[32]

(13) The writer of the following is one of our most respected historians:

> Ellen White presented the sublime beauty of Jesus Christ and then, in stark contrast, the evidence that leadership, laity, institutions, conferences, mission fields, and the church as a whole, were desperately in need of reformation. Over and over she

stressed that "not a few, but *many*" (emphasis hers) have been losing their spiritual zeal and turning away from the light. ... Leaders in Battle Creek have turned their backs to the Lord; many church members also have rejected His lordship and chosen Baal's instead. Conference presidents are behaving like medieval bishops, while "whole conferences" and "every institution" are being perverted with the same principles. Some leaders actually "boast" that they will not follow the testimonies. A "strange blindness!" has come upon the General Conference president so that even he is acting contrary to the light. So serious is the situation at the publishing house in Battle Creek that "all heaven is indignant." Indeed, the Lord "has a controversy with His people."[33]

(14) In 1891 the General Conference virtually exiled her to Australia, thus ensuring the final defeat of the "beginning" of the latter rain and the loud cry. She had no light from the Lord that she should go. In 1896 she wrote plaintively to the General Conference president:

> The Lord was not in our leaving America. He did not reveal that it was His will that I should leave Battle Creek. The Lord did not plan this, but He let you all move after your own imaginings. The Lord would have had [us] ... remain in America. We were needed at the heart of the work, and had your spiritual perception discerned the true situation, you would never have consented to the movement made. ... There was so great a willingness to have us leave, that the Lord permitted this thing to take place. Those who were weary of the testimonies borne were left without the persons who bore them. Our separation from Battle Creek was to let men have their own will and way. ... Had you stood in the right position the move would not have been made at that time. The Lord would have worked for Australia by other means, and a strong influence would have been held at Battle Creek, the great heart of the work. ... It was not the Lord who devised this matter. ... When we left, relief was felt by many, but not so much by yourself, and the Lord was displeased, for He had set us to stand at the wheels of the moving machinery at Battle Creek.[34]

(15) Shortly after she was sent to Australia, E. J. Waggoner was packed off to England. According to Ellen White, there is evidence that this was also in the nature of an exile.[35]

(16) She finally returned to her homeland to attend the 1901 General Conference. She called for reformation, revival, and reorganization. The reorganization took place, and on the surface a reformation and revival seemed to be under way. But she was forced later to declare that the latter was not deep and thorough. On January 5, 1903, she wrote her poignant "What Might Have Been," lamenting in "an agony of disappointment" that the spiritual revival/reformation "at the last General Conference" was only a dream, "not a reality."[36]

After the close of the session she wrote to Dr. Kellogg, "What a wonderful work could have been done for the vast company gathered in Battle Creek at the General Conference of 1901 … but … the leaders closed and bolted the door against the Spirit's entrance."[37]

Whether "the leaders" she had in mind were Kellogg and his cohorts, or the total leadership including the General Conference, has been debated. But she wrote to a friend a few months later, indicating that the problem was indeed with the total leadership. At least it seems difficult to understand her in any other way:

> The result of the last General Conference has been the greatest, the most terrible sorrow of my life. No change was made. The spirit that should have been brought into the whole work as the result of that meeting, was not brought in because men did not receive the testimonies of the Spirit of God. As they went to their several fields of labor, they did not walk in the light that the Lord had flashed upon their pathway, but carried into their work the wrong principles that had been prevailing in the work at Battle Creek.
>
> The Lord has marked every movement made by the leading men in our institutions and conferences.[38]

A Question That Troubles Many Adventists

If the 1888 message was all that good, why did the two 1888 messengers lose their way? Was there error in the message that led them astray?

The safest way to answer is to let the lady speak. There was nothing wrong in their message itself:

> If Satan can impress the mind and stir up the passions of those who claim to believe the truth, and … get them to commit themselves to the wrong side, he has laid his plans to lead them on a long journey.… There seems to be no other course for them except to go on, believing they are right in their bitterness of feeling toward their brethren [Jones and Waggoner]. Will the Lord's messenger bear the pressure brought against him? If so, it is because God bids him stand in His strength and vindicate the truth that he is sent of God.…

> There has been a determined effort to make of no effect the message God has sent. … Should the Lord's messengers, after standing manfully for the truth for a time, fall under temptation, and dishonor Him who has given them their work, will that be proof that the message is not true? No, because the Bible is true. … Sin on the part of the messenger of God would cause Satan to rejoice, and those who have rejected the messenger and the message would triumph.[39]

But why should the messengers "fall under temptation"? We must face reality: their losing their way was largely *our* fault, "ours" who constitute the body. For some important reason the Lord permitted the two to fail in their trial. Speaking of their opposers, she said:

> To be suspicious, watching for a chance and greedily seizing upon it to prove that those brethren … are not sound in the faith. There is danger that this course of action will produce the very result assumed; and to a great degree the guilt will rest upon those who are watching for evil.[40]

The same sad process worked in Dr. Kellogg's heart, weakening him spiritually so that he fell under temptations that came later.[41] Satan had a field day. After leading "us" "to a great degree" to "produce" Jones and Waggoner's stumbling, he has now employed that very tragedy to induce us over a century later to suspect their message to be an insidious evil.[42] This is one of the most skillful movements ever devised in history: the actual "beginning" of the latter rain and the loud cry must now be feared as dangerous!

But Ellen White made it very clear that this position is not only a minor historical error, but it is "a fatal delusion":

> Some of our brethren … are full of jealousy and evil surmising, and are ever ready to show in just what way they differ with Elder Jones or Waggoner. The same spirit that was manifested in the past manifests itself at every opportunity [this is after the confessions]. … It is quite possible that Elder Jones or Waggoner may be overthrown by the temptations of the enemy; but if they should be, this would not prove that they had no message from God. … But should this happen, how many would take this position, and enter into a fatal delusion because they are not under the control of the Spirit of God. … I know that this is the very position many would take if either of these men were to fall.[43]

Astounding as it may seem, this spirit of enmity was the same that moved the Duke of Alva and others to oppose the Protestants in an earlier age. Ellen White plainly called it "persecution," and compared its spirit to that of the Papacy:

> You have thought you could see inconsistencies in A. T. Jones and E. J. Waggoner. … It is the work of Satan to cause alienation. He knows that it will separate brethren from one another, and more than this, separate them from God. … A fierce and determined spirit … will place the brother in a position that hurts his influence. … Upon whom does the hurt come? Upon the Son of the infinite God. …
>
> The hatred of evil against good exists as surely now as in the days of Christ when the multitudes cried, "Away with him!" … Cease to war against those of your own faith. … The first thing recorded in Scripture history after the fall was the persecution of Abel. And the last thing in Scripture prophecy is the persecution against

those who refuse to receive the mark of the beast. We should be the last people on the earth to indulge in the slightest degree the spirit of persecution against those who are bearing the message of God to the world. This is the most terrible feature of unchristlikeness that has manifested itself among us since the Minneapolis meeting.[44]

I have been shown that [the Minneapolis opposition] was the same ruling spirit that was revealed in the condemnation of Christ. When the Papists were in controversy with men who took their stand on the Bible for proof of doctrines they considered it a matter that only death could settle. I could see a similar spirit cherished in the hearts of our brethren, and I would not give room to it for an hour.[45]

Martin Luther had it easy compared to our 1888 messengers. The pope's fulminations meant nothing to him so long as he could turn to Daniel 7 and recognize the papacy as "the little horn." But Jones and Waggoner had firm faith that the Seventh-day Adventist Church is the true remnant church, the last among the "seven golden candlesticks." How could they understand this phenomenal enmity against the message of Christ's much more abounding grace? The strain was too much for their human nature to bear; evidence indicates that Jones lost the true balance of his mind.[46]

The Story of Christ's Unrequited Love

The true story of 1888 is one of deep-hearted unbelief as serious as that of the Jews who rejected Christ long ago.[47] But there is good news in the story. "The gifts and calling of God are irrevocable."[48]

Even if His people are not faithful, He must remain faithful. He must await the coming of a generation who will humble their hearts and believe Him. Christ has not abandoned Laodicea; He is still standing outside the door, knocking. Although His presence is not inside, it is a vast encouragement that He still wants in!

The story is most clearly seen as unrequited love. The language in Revelation 3:20 is a direct quotation from the Greek of the Septuagint Song of Solomon 5:2-6 where Christ ties in the experience of the remnant church with that "song" of the Disappointed Lover. He knocks at the gate but is selfishly denied entry by the one who is the only true object of His love. "She" was foolish not to let Him in when He knocked over a century ago; but she is honest in heart, and *she must and will come to her time of repentance.*

Thank God that Satan's victory was not total! The finishing of the gospel commission has been long delayed, but confrontation with truth gives us a new opportunity for repentance. The full story may humble our pride, but it will strengthen our faith.[49]

The honor and vindication of Christ require our repentance. The evidence indicates that the Lord gives a given generation only one chance to accept the precious gift of the latter rain, as He gave the generation of Israelites coming out of Egypt only one chance (Kadesh-Barnea) to enter their Promised Land. In both instances, rebellious unbelief conclusively delayed the work of God.

The Lord's servant has questioned "whether genuine rebellion is ever curable."[50] History seems to say that repentance must be effected by a new generation, unless this one chooses to repent.

Before the new generation could enter Canaan under Joshua, they had to have their Book of Deuteronomy. They must thoroughly understand the preceding generation's rebellion and repent of it in a corporate sense. Only a repentant people could enter Canaan. It was not *they* who had rebelled at Kadesh-Barnea (they were too young); but they had to repent of *their parents'* rebellion, for Moses told them repeatedly that *they* were the ones who had rebelled. It doesn't make sense unless you see the corporate relationship.

Likewise, before modern Israel can again receive the outpouring of the latter rain and proclaim the loud cry message, they must thoroughly understand the truth of a previous generation's rejection of the same blessing they now seek—our new Deuteronomy experience. This is corporate and denominational repentance.

The Secret of the 1888 Opposition

The one who stands back in the shadows of the 1888 opposition is, of course, the great dragon of Revelation 12:17. This brings to view his last battle in the great controversy. His opposition *from within* centers on "the testimony of Jesus Christ," the Spirit of Prophecy.[51] From *without,* it's on the commandments of God.

Seventh-day Adventists have always recognized that "the spirit of prophecy" given to the apostolic church has been manifested in the ministry of Ellen White.[52] The unreasonable, persistent opposition against her for all these years marks its source as from that "dragon." This reached a climax in our 1888 experience. The full reality of what she wrote must be appreciated (we quote several statements herewith):

> "Again and again did I bear my testimony to those assembled [at Minneapolis] but that testimony was not received." "The Lord had [a blessing] for us at Minneapolis … but there was no reception. Some received the light for the people and rejoiced in it. Then there were others that stood right back, and *their position* has given confidence to others to talk unbelief." "Leading men are giving a mold to the work that will result in a loss of many souls." "The Spirit of God has been present in power among His people, but it could not be bestowed upon them, because they did not open their hearts to receive it." "Those in responsible positions in Battle Creek … have rejected light. … They have interposed themselves between the heaven-sent light and the people."[53]

The special message the Lord Jesus addresses us (Revelation 3:14-21) indicates it is related to our history.[54] The import of the original escaped the translators: "You say, I am rich and I *have been enriched.*" The original language pinpoints our claims in our denominational history. We have been enriched by an *acceptance* of the message that was to illuminate the earth with glory and prepare that generation for translation! Yet no one has been translated, and the loud cry has not yet lighted the earth. This means either one of two things: the message was not what Ellen White said it was, *or our acceptance of it was not what we have supposed it was.*

Understanding Brings Hope For the Future

Only if we reject truth can *good* news become bad news. We can surrender all false ideas in exchange for truth like we exchange money for something we "buy." Maybe that's why the Lord says, *"Buy* of Me gold ... and white raiment."

If we will listen to Christ's voice and believe what He says, the long-awaited blessings of the latter rain and the loud cry can become reality *in this generation.* The power was inherent in the objective message itself, and thank God, we can recover it.

Doesn't the hungry world desperately need the spiritual food entrusted to us a century ago?

Chapter Ten Endnotes

[1] 1 Corinthians 1:29.

[2] E. G White, *Review and Herald,* September 16, 1902.

[3] John and Elizabeth Sherrill, *The Hiding Place* (Chosen Books).

[4] Edith Hamilton in *Saturday Evening Post,* September 27, 1958.

[5] *Testimonies to Ministers,* pp. 91, 97; 1896.

[6] *Early Writings,* p. 271.

[7] *Review and Herald,* March 18, May 27, 1890; MS 15, 1888; Letter 77, January 9, 1893 [1126].

[8] Cf. MS 24, 1888; *Selected Messages,* Book Three, p. 174; *Fundamentals of Christian Education,* p. 472; Letters 13, 51A, 1895 (A. V. Olson, *Through Crisis to Victory,* pp. 119, 124).

[9] Letter B21, 1888 [86].

[10] MS 9, 1888.

[11] MS 15, 1888.

[12] C. C. McReynolds, D. File 189, Ellen G. White Estate.

[13] R. T. Nash, "Eyewitness Report of the 1888 General Conference."

[14] W. W. Prescott, *General Conference Bulletin,* 1901, p. 321.

[15] A. G. Daniells, *Christ Our Righteousness,* p. 47; 1926.

[16] A. W. Spalding, *Origin and History of Seventh-day Adventists,* Vol. 2, pp. 295, 297.

[17] A. T. Jones, *General Conference Bulletin,* 1893, p. 183.

[18] Letter 184, 1901; *Evangelism,* p. 696; cf. "a long journey," Letter O19d, 1892 [1023].

[19] *Selected Messages,* Book One, pp. 234, 235; 1896.

[20] Letter O43a, 1890 [752, 753].

[21] MS 30, 1889 [360].

[22] Letters C-14, 1889 [314, 320], S24, 1892 [1043].

[23] *Review and Herald,* March 11, 18, 1890.

Chapter Ten Endnotes (*Continued*)

[24] *Adventist Review,* October 30, 1986.

[25] Letter U3, 1889 [252].

[26] Letter 77, 1893 [1122, 1125].

[27] Letter B2a, November 5, 1892 [1067, 1069]. Many statements Ellen White made subsequent to 1892 confirm that her expression "not one" is the truth.

[28] *General Conference Bulletin,* p. 23.

[29] *Ibid.,* p. 205.

[30] Letter to A. O. Tait, August 27, 1896 [1608].

[31] Letter, May 31, 1896 [1568].

[32] Letter E51, 1897.

[33] Mervyn Maxwell, *Tell It to the World,* pp. 246, 247.

[34] Letter 127, 1896 [1622-1624].

[35] W. C. White letter to A. G. Daniells, May 30, 1902.

[36] Cf. *Testimonies,* Vol. 8, pp. 104-106.

[37] Letter, August 5, 1902.

[38] Letter to Judge Jesse Arthur, January 15, 1903.

[39] Letter O19d, 1892 [1022-1025].

[40] Letter January 9, 1893 (*General Conference Bulletin,* 1893, pp. 419-421 [1127]).

[41] Letter B21, 1888 [100-102]; MS 13, 1901.

[42] Cf. George Knight, *From 1888 to Apostasy, passim* (Review and Herald, 1987).

[43] Letter S24, 1892 [1042-1045].

[44] Letter 25b, 1892 [1012, 1013]. See also MS13, 1889 [516, 517].

[45] MS 13, 1889 [516].

[46] Letter 104, 1911.

[47] Cf. MS 9, 1888, *Through Crisis to Victory,* p. 292; MS 15, 1888, *ibid.,* pp. 297, 300; MS 13, 1889; *Review and Herald,* March 4, 11, August 26, 1890; April 11, 18, 1893; *Testimonies to Ministers,* pp. 64, 75-80, etc.

[48] Romans 11:29.

[49] It is a humbling experience to read the full collection of Ellen White's writings concerning 1888, in the four volumes of 1821 pages.

[50] *Selected Messages,* Book Two, p. 393.

[51] Verse 17, last part; Revelation 19:10.

[52] See 1 Corinthians 12:28; Ephesians 4:8-12.

[53] See the Appendix of *Through Crisis to Victory 1888-1901* for Ellen White's Minneapolis sermons; *Testimonies to Ministers,* pp. 63-81, 89-98; *Selected Messages,* Book One, pp. 234, 235; *ibid.,* Book Three, pp. 163-189.

[54] Revelation 3:14-17.

Chapter Eleven

WILL THE SEVENTH-DAY ADVENTIST CHURCH EVER BECOME BABYLON?

This is perhaps the most serious of all the topics we have looked at in this essay.

Many say they like Jesus and they like the Bible, but they have no use for "organized religion." We now face a "vegetarian" version of this within the Seventh-day Adventist Church—people who like the Bible and the Spirit of Prophecy, but are doubtful about the "organized church."

Some darkly hint that the church has become "Babylon" in defiance of Ellen White's testimony to the contrary.[1] To them church membership seems passé. Because of its problems the Lord has probably forsaken the organized church or will do so, they say. Such usually gravitate into off-shoots, withdrawing support from the denomination.

Those so willing frequently quote a statement from Ellen White's *Acts of the Apostles,* page 11, that seems to encourage them. We will use italics for the much-quoted excerpt:

The church is God's fortress, His city of refuge, which He holds in a revolted world. Any betrayal of the church is treachery to Him who has bought mankind with the blood of His only-begotten Son. From the beginning, *faithful souls have constituted the church on earth.*

This is understood to say, "From the beginning, the true church has been constituted of unorganized, disjointed, uncoordinated, 'faithful souls.' Denominational organization must fail." But does it say that?

What is the church? Is the organized church a *Titanic* doomed to sink? Should "faithful souls" abandon it and get a life raft on their own?

Will there be no "ship" in the last days? Is the true church merely a non-cohesive, unorganized scattering of "faithful souls"?

The context of this statement seems to make that difficult to believe. It says the church is a cohesive, *organized body*—a "fortress" and a "city of refuge." In the Bible, a "city" is always an organized, corporate body of people. To forsake that organized church and withdraw support from it is so serious that it is called "treachery to Christ." If the church is to become the Bride of Christ, He must be rather jealous for her.

How can we know the truth? The answer comes by asking one significant question: What is the mind of Christ toward the organized Seventh-day Adventist Church? That is what we seek to know.

Has the Lord's Church Always Been an Organized Body?

The beginnings of the true church can be traced to the everlasting (or new) covenant that the Lord made with Abraham long ago:

> "Get out of your country,
> From your kindred
> And from your father's house,
> To a land that I will show you.
> I will make you a *great nation*. ...
> And in you all the families of the earth shall be blessed."[2]

Thus the Lord began to organize His people to be a denominated, visible family, a "nation." His purpose: that they witness in the world.

Abraham's descendants were elected to be the ancient equivalent of today's organized church. They were publicly to share and exemplify his faith. Their nationhood was to demonstrate that it is possible for human beings to function in an organized unity, perfectly devoted to the Lord's guidance.

That nation came to be known as Israel. Her history records a series of ups and downs, with many dark episodes of corporate failure. (The "downs" were the direct result of the old covenant idea they had embraced on their own.) But did her terrible backslidings, such as in the days of Elijah and Jeremiah, cancel the original election of God? The answer has to be no.

Although they were severely punished for their apostasies (especially Baal-worship), neither Israel nor Judah ever *became* Babylon. Even while they were captives *in* Babylon they remained Israel. Baal-worship was a disease that afflicted the body but did not transform it into Babylon.

Even in Israel's darkest hours, she was still the brightest spot in a darker world. For example, Daniel and his companions accomplished in Babylonian exile what the kings and priests of Judah had failed to do in their national prosperity. At the nadir of Judah's terrible unfaithfulness to God, when the prospects for reformation seemed darkest, Jeremiah bought land at Anathoth, demonstrating his faith in the future healing of the apostasy.[3] In all His wrath with His faithless people God remembered mercy and loyalty to them.[4]

His faithfulness to His promise does not excuse the faith-lessness of His people today, but it points to His divine solution to the problems of apostasy and worldliness in His church, a solution that gives hope when all else seems hopeless. (We will consider later what is this solution.)

Who Is "Israel" Today?

It is generally agreed among us that the modern Seventh-day Adventist Church has seriously repeated the history of ancient Israel. As we saw in our last chapter, Ellen White often said that our "in-a-great-measure" rejection of the 1888 message over a century ago was a replay of the Jews' rejection of Christ.[5]

When they finally crucified Him and rejected His apostles in 34 A.D., while the Lord did not abandon His original covenant, He permitted a "shaking" to test His professed people. Two groups became distinguished and separated. The believing ones among them remained as His true church, and the unbelievers were *shaken out*. To the unbelieving Jews the Lord had to say, "The kingdom of God will be taken from you and given to a nation bearing the fruits of it."[6] The "nation" was the church continuing as the true Israel.

From the beginning, Abraham's *true* "seed" were never merely natural descendants. Not in Ishmael but "in Isaac shall thy seed be called."[7] Righteousness by faith was as true in Abraham's day as in Paul's. Isaiah saw ahead of time what would happen in Israel's final test:

> "It shall come to pass
> That the glory of Jacob will wane,
> And the fatness of his flesh grow lean. . . .
> Yet gleaning grapes will be left in it,
> Like the shaking of an olive tree,
> Two or three olives at the top of the uppermost bough,
> Four or five in its most fruitful branches,"
> Says the Lord God of Israel.[8]

In 34 A. D. the physical nation of Israel was rejected, but the true Israel repented at Pentecost because of faith in Christ, for "if you are Christ's, then you are Abraham's seed, and heirs according to the promise."[9] That's how these contrite believers became the new Israel, the church, the true "nation bearing the fruits." The church was not an appendage or off-shoot from Israel; *it was the true descendants of Abraham.*[10]

What Created The "Shaking"?

We have frequently heard a popular saying that the church will never experience repentance and reformation until persecution hits us. But the test for ancient Israel was not brought about by external force from the Roman Empire but by the gospel. What brought the nation to her final crisis was the life and death of Christ and the apostles' clear testimony at Pentecost of what it all means.

Likewise, it will be a revelation of the truth of righteousness by faith that precipitates the final shaking today, not persecution from the world. The Lord will do the work, not Satan. Persecution will come, but it's impossible that a *lukewarm* church can be persecuted by Satan. He wants to keep that church lukewarm! Only those "who live godly in Christ Jesus" *can* be persecuted.

At the beginning of His ministry Christ selected disciples and ordained them, disciplining them to proclaim the gospel to the world. "'He ordained twelve.'... The first step was now to be taken in the organization of the church that after Christ's departure was to be His representative on earth."[11] "On this rock [their expressed faith in Him] I will build My church, and the gates of Hades shall not prevail against it."[12] He commissioned them to be a disciplined, unified "body": "As the Father has sent Me, I also send you."[13] They were not a disjointed, quadriplegic scattering of "faithful souls."

The Holy Spirit continued to organize and to lead the members toward perfect unity and cohesion. Here's an example of how He did it:

> The Holy Spirit said, "Now separate to Me Barnabas and Saul for the work to which I have called them." Then, having fasted and prayed, and laid hands on them, they sent them away.[14]

There's good news here: the apostles and church elders were responsive to the Holy Spirit's leading. But our 1888 history is different from that of the apostles. What "the Holy Spirit said" to us we *didn't* do! But now the time has come when we must respond as promptly to His leading as the apostles did. If the Lord has to coerce us into His kingdom dragging our feet, kicking and holding back every step of the way, how can this bring Him honor and glory?

The same Holy Spirit who organized the apostles is still alive today. We read that Paul left Titus "in Crete, that you should set in order the things that are lacking, and appoint elders in every city as I commanded you."[15] This was the pattern.

When problems threatened, "it pleased the apostles and elders, with the whole church" to convene the first general council to discuss the issues openly, and unitedly to seek the Holy Spirit's solution. There was no "kingly power" to dictate what should be done. The "Jerusalem decree" was the work of lay members and apostles praying together, "the whole church" studying and discussing.[16]

Even during the persecution of the Dark Ages evidence shows that the true church was visible and organized. The messages to the angels of "the seven churches" of Revelation 2 and 3 indicate that the apostles' pattern continued. Many of the records of those churches were destroyed by their enemies, but sufficient have survived to show that the "faithful souls" of the Dark Ages were coordinated as a "body."

Inspiration likens the true church of medieval times to a "woman" in "the wilderness," a symbol of an organized body.[17] "There existed for many centuries *bodies of Christians* who remained almost wholly free from papal corruption. ... The Vaudois churches, in their purity and simplicity, resembled the church of apostolic times."[18] In fact, Christ makes a complaint against "the church of Thyatira," the church in the wilderness, because they were not intradisciplined enough—they permitted "Jezebel" to teach in their midst.[19] This implies the normal presence of order and corporate responsibility.

What Keeps the Church Together

Christ's organization of His church is different from any business or political entity. Paul's idea in 1 Corinthians 12 is brilliant: "As the body is one and has many members, but all the members of that one body, being many are one body, so also is Christ. ... You are the body of Christ, and members individually."[20] A "body" is not an unco-ordinated, scattered mélange of dismembered organs, an eye here and a nose there, and a stomach somewhere else. Each "member" is joined to the other and to the head.

When the early church functioned as a body in disciplined coordination under the guidance of the Holy Spirit, the Lord respected its organization. For example, when Saul of Tarsus was converted, the Lord brought him into immediate fellowship with His organized church.[21]

The idea is beautiful Good News. Christ being the "head," each believer is automatically an important and functioning member of the body. No political or other human organization can enjoy such perfect unity where each member sees himself as especially created to fill a need. Talk about self-esteem! Nothing nurtures it like living member-ship in the "body of Christ." Every believing person discovers therein to his everlasting joy his true sense of self-identity and fulfillment.

Over a hundred years after Minneapolis and 1888, the time has come for us to fulfill Paul's vision of a perfectly coordinated church where every member feels needed. For nearly two thousand years Paul's picture of genuine, lasting "church growth" has been awaiting its full realization:

We should no longer be children, tossed to and fro and carried about with every wind of doctrine, … but speaking the truth in love [*agape*], may grow up in all things into Him who is the head—Christ—from whom the whole body, joined and knit together by what every joint supplies, according to the effective working by which every part does its share, causes growth of the body for the edifying [building up] of itself in love [*agape*].[22]

It's natural for some to fear that the church and its institutions are now too big and complicated ever to be successful. But the Bible gives no hint that the growth of the body makes difficult or impossible the Holy Spirit's work. Overall, the idea is that what will unify the church is pure, unadulterated truth promulgated wholeheartedly and unreservedly by its leadership. What happened in 1888 must be replayed, but this time in sanctified reverse.

The Organization of the Seventh-day Adventist Church

The Holy Spirit led our Seventh-day Adventist pioneers to organize:

We sought the Lord with earnest prayer. … Light was given by His Spirit that there must be order and thorough discipline in the church—that organization was essential. … Notwithstanding that the Lord gave testimony after testimony upon this point, the opposition was strong, and it had to be met again and again. … We engaged in the work of organization, and marked prosperity attended this advance movement.[23]

Now we ask, What is the mind of Christ today toward the organized denomination known as Seventh-day Adventists? Can we know for sure?

In the last book of the Bible we can trace His mind toward His church and its destiny from the apostles down to the end of the world. In Revelation 12 He pictures the church as "a woman" opposed by Satan through all the Christian era. The church in the last days emerges in the final act as "the remnant of her seed" (KJV) which "keep the commandments of God and have the testimony of Jesus Christ."[24] Her magnificent destiny is to become the Bride of Christ. The time must come when "the marriage of the Lamb has come, and His wife has made herself ready."[25] It was God's intention that 1888 be that time of betrothal.

Thus the outstanding demonstration of this two thousand years of history is the public display of a world church that is as completely loyal to Christ as a loving, faithful bride is loyal to her husband.

Since the true Head of this church is Christ Himself, His honor and vindication are involved. Let's not give up hope; He knows a way to bring healing and unity to His "body."

Ellen White is clear. She identifies the organized Seventh-day Adventist Church as this "remnant":

> In a special sense Seventh-day Adventists have been set in the world as watchmen and light-bearers. To them has been entrusted the last warning for a perishing world, … [the] proclamation of the first, second, and third angels' messages. … The most solemn truths ever entrusted to mortals have been given us to proclaim to the world.[26]

> Let us have faith that God is going to carry the noble ship which bears the people of God safely into port.[27]

> I had an impressive dream last night. I thought that you were on a strong vessel, sailing on very rough waters. Sometimes the waves beat over the top, and you were drenched with water. You said, "I shall get off; this vessel is going down." "No," said one who appeared to be the captain, "this vessel sails into the harbor. She will never go down."[28]

> The church may appear as about to fall, but it does not fall. It remains, while the sinners in Zion will be sifted out—the chaff separated from the precious wheat. This is a terrible ordeal, but nevertheless it must take place.[29]

> I am instructed to say to Seventh-day Adventists the world over, God has called us as a people to be a peculiar treasure unto

Himself. He has appointed that His church on earth shall stand perfectly united in the Spirit and counsel of the Lord of hosts to the end of time.[30]

Some of these and other similar statements were made decades after the 1888 experience, indicating that Ellen White still regarded the organized church as the body of Christ, enfeebled and defective as it was. *But it must experience repentance and spiritual reformation.*

How has Christ regarded this organized church? As He called Abraham and his descendants to witness to His truth in a world of paganism, so He has called Seventh-day Adventists to witness to the apostate Christian churches and to the entire world, including Judaism, Islam, Hinduism, Buddhism, and paganism.

Who Is the True Leadership of This Church?

(1) If it is a fallible hierarchy of men and women, there is no hope for its future, and likewise no hope for any off-shoot from it to succeed any better.

(2) But if we have a firm faith that the Lord Jesus is the true Leader of this church, then we can have confidence that He will cleanse and purify it as He has promised to do. If it was the Lord Jesus who initiated this church's calling, we can be sure that He knows how to see it through.

(3) The mind of Christ toward the Seventh-day Adventist Church is not impossible to know. It's in His message in Revelation 3:14-21. No way does He reveal Himself as being indulgent and lackadaisical toward our backslidings and failures. He is a "Faithful and True Witness," straight-forward, direct in correcting His people. He says He is so nauseated with their lukewarmness that He feels like throwing up (this is what the Greek of verse 16 actually says).

He tells them that they are "wretched, miserable, poor, blind, and naked," with the little Greek word *ho* meaning that of all the seven churches of history they are *the* one outstandingly so.

(4) But His loyalty is revealed in intimate family-love, the kind that cannot be misunderstood even when family members severely chasten each other: "As many as I love (*phileo*), I rebuke and chasten." His solution to our denominational problems: "Be zealous and repent."[31]

(5) The prophecy calls for a people to be raised up in the last days who fulfill the will of God and bring honor and glory to the Lamb. They will provide a convincing answer to the long-delayed Lord's prayer, "Thy will be done in earth, as it is in heaven." They share executive authority with Christ in the conclusion of the great controversy, "Cabinet members," if you please.[32] Their loyalty to Christ in no way merits salvation; but it gives convincing evidence that the gospel has the power Christ claims for it.

The Lord Himself has denominated that people to be Seventh-day Adventists. The dragon has developed a special "rage," highly refined, a massive "inside job" of inducing discouragement and disloyalty in the hearts of conscientious church members. Some wounded ones believe themselves to have been persecuted by the church, not realizing that the true source is the "dragon" trying to usurp the place of Christ in his final "war" with the remnant. The ancient patriarch Job had difficulty knowing who was tormenting him. He thought it was the Lord when in fact it was Satan. It is possible for us also to be confused.

Our failures and backslidings have indeed been grievous, so much so that Satan claims them as evidence that Christ has abandoned the church, and some have bought the idea. Yet the Lord can heal our back-slidings.[33] To human judgment the church may *appear* to be a vast graveyard of dry bones without life. But the Lord can and will resurrect them. "Behold, he who keeps Israel shall neither slumber nor sleep."[34] The Lord has not forgotten this world and its needs. He "is at the head of the work, and He will set everything in order. If matters need adjusting at the head of the work, God will attend to that, and work to right every wrong."[35] That's a truth for us to believe!

But Can God Do All That on His Own?

The Lord needs human agents through whom He can work to "set everything in order." It is not His plan to work independently of them. It is not fair for us to pray, "Lord, will *You* please do something," and then sit back ourselves *and do nothing*.

Through close fellowship with Him, those who are "crucified with Christ" will "sit" with Him in His throne and share with Him the executive authority of working "to right every wrong."[36] The cowardly, proud love of self has been taken to the cross, and the overcomers know the reality of what John means when he says, "Perfect love (*agape*) casts out fear."[37]

They are not made of sterner or better stuff than others; they have simply seen something that others have not seen—the reality of the cross of Christ. This is true faith, and it has nerved them to stand for the right wherever they are, even though the heavens fall. They are the true Israel who exercise the faith of Abraham.

In a word, it is genuine righteousness by faith that has transformed these naturally timid, shy people into brave Christlike servants of truth. "The one who is feeble among them in that day shall be as David."[38] It has also transformed those whose natural love of self makes them arrogant, abrasive, and pushy, so that "the love (*agape*) of Christ constrains" them to demonstrate His meekness and gentleness:

> From the light I have, I know that Satan is trying to bring in that which will make people think they have a wonderful work to do. But when God gives a man a message, that man, by his meekness and lowliness, will give evidence that God is working through him. God lives and reigns, and He desires us to walk before Him in humility. He does not wish this man N to force himself before a congregation. ...

> We are not going to be interrupted in meeting after meeting by those who claim they have a message to deliver. He who presses himself forward into a place where he is not wanted is not doing the work of God. We are to work like soldiers in an army. We are not to step out of the ranks, and begin to work on our own account.[39]

The Holy Spirit has not gone to sleep. He will manifest Himself in a message of truth that is so clear and powerful and so self-humbling that fanaticism and arrogance on the one hand and timidity on the other will vanish before it:

> Amid the confusing cries, "Lo, here is Christ! Lo, there is Christ!" will be borne a special testimony, a special message of truth appropriate for this time, which message is to be received, believed, and acted upon. It is the truth, not fanciful ideas, that is

efficacious. The eternal truth of the Word will stand forth free from all seductive errors and spiritualistic interpretations, free from all fancifully drawn, alluring pictures. Falsehoods will be urged upon the attention of God's people, but the truth is to stand clothed in its beautiful, pure garments, ... uncontaminated by the fallacies by which Satan seeks to deceive, if possible, the very elect.[40]

Abraham, "the father of the faithful," had to learn to have the faith the Lord has—a faith that "gives life to the dead and calls those things which do not exist as though they did."[41] So must we. Where we see only dry bones, we must exercise the faith to call "those things which do not exist [apparently] as though they did," and thus make possible the Lord's miracle of a new creation, a resurrection from death to spiritual life.

Even if there were not even one faithful Seventh-day Adventist in all the world, he who has the faith of Abraham will believe that the prophecies of Revelation concerning the remnant church must be fulfilled. *He will cooperate with the Lord's work of resurrecting dry bones so that that which does not exist will be.*

But in actual fact, it does already exist, for as in Elijah's day, there are "seven thousand" who do not bow the knee to Baal. They may appear to be hidden, and they may seem cowardly silent in the crisis; but they await only the revelation of the full truth of righteousness by faith to support fully and fearlessly its regenerating, life-giving work. The problem is self; and self will be crucified with Christ when righteousness by faith is finally understood.

The Lord needs millions of "Elijahs" who will lovingly yet firmly stand for the right, who have received and appreciated that *agape* which casts out fear. Each will bloom where providence has planted him, in committees, on church boards, in conference administration, in the classroom, or in the church pew.

Will the Past History Of Apostasy and Failure Always Repeat Itself?

If the answer is yes, we face nothing but hopeless despair for the future.

Even if a pure and holy off-shoot should develop, for God to be fair He must give it time also to grow big and wealthy and succumb to temptation and fail as have all "righteous" movements in the past. If the cycle of failure and apostasy in the organized church is endless, all "reformers" and their organized institutions are likewise doomed to ultimate failure, given enough time. But "present truth" is better news than that.

The foundation text of the Seventh-day Adventist Church declares that for once in history, history will not be repeated: *"Unto two thousand and three hundred days* [years]; *then shall the sanctuary be cleansed."*[42] That cleansing or making right has never yet in history taken place for the *body* of the church. In order for the heavenly sanctuary to be cleansed, the Lord's sanctuary on earth must first be cleansed. The books of heaven can never record the "blotting out of sins" until this work is first accomplished in the hearts of His people on earth. Those heavenly records will never tell a lie. Speaking in context of the 1888 message, Ellen White emphasizes some wonderfully Good News:

> Christ is in the heavenly sanctuary, and he is there to make an atonement for the people. He is there to present his wounded side and pierced hands to his Father. He is there to plead for his Church that is upon the earth. He is cleansing the sanctuary from the sins of the people. What is our work?—It is our work to be in harmony with the work of Christ. By faith we are to work with him, to be in union with him.[43]

> While Christ is cleansing the sanctuary, the worshippers on earth should carefully review their life, and compare their character with the standard of righteousness. As they see their defects they should seek the aid of the Spirit of God to enable them to have moral strength to resist the temptations of Satan, and to reach the perfection of the standard. They may be victors over the very temptations which seemed too strong for humanity to bear; for the divine power will be combined with their human effort, and Satan cannot overcome them.[44]

The One who will accomplish that amazing task is the High Priest. His business is that of being a Savior from sin. It's His job to cleanse the sanctuary, not ours; but it's our job to cooperate with Him, to let Him do it, to stop hindering Him "in His office work":

> We are in the day of atonement, and we are to work in harmony with Christ's work of cleansing the sanctuary from the sins of the people. Let no man who desires to be found with the wedding garment on, resist our Lord in his office work.[45]

No material or sensual delight the world can offer can compare with the thrill of cooperating with that heavenly High Priest!

Let us spend our lifetime energies and all that we have in working with Him. God grant that never under any circumstances or under any pressure may we let ourselves work at cross purposes with Him.

To put the "1888" story into a simple nutshell:

In 1888 the Bridegroom-to-be approached the "woman" whom He loved, His intended Bride-to-be, to pledge to Him her tryst. The Song of Solomon chapter 5:1-7 describes what happened in dramatic symbolism.

We read of His plight. Lonely, hungry, drenched with the rain, He knocks patiently at her door (*epi ten thuran*, Greek, LXX; Jesus quotes it in His message to "the angel of the church of the Laodiceans, the leadership of His last-days' church).

But she is thinking only of herself, her own comfort. But as He continues knocking, century after century, finally she comes to her senses; finally she stops thinking of herself and thinks of Him still outside "the door," lonely, and hurt, the only One who truly loves her.

And at last she gets up and goes to let Him in.

Chapter Eleven Endnotes

[1] Cf. *Testimonies to Ministers,* pp. 32-62.
[2] Genesis 12:1-3.
[3] Cf. Jeremiah 32.
[4] See Jeremiah 16:14, 15; 23:3-8; 30:18-31:37.
[5] Cf. *Special Testimonies,* Series A, No. 6, p. 20; January 16, 1896. Stated over a hundred times!
[6] Matthew 21:43.
[7] Romans 9:7.
[8] Isaiah 17:4-6.
[9] Galatians 3:29.
[10] Daniel 9:24; Matthew 21:42-45; Luke 20:16; Acts 13:46; Romans 9:7, 8; 11:17, 25- 27.
[11] *The Desire of Ages,* p. 291.
[12] Matthew 16:18.
[13] John 20:21-23.
[14] Acts 13:1-4.
[15] Titus 1:5-11.
[16] See Acts 15:1-29.
[17] Revelation 12:6.
[18] *The Great Controversy,* pp. 63, 69.
[19] Revelation 2:18-20.
[20] Vss. 12, 27.
[21] Acts 9:10-19; see also *Acts of the Apostles,* pp. 122, 163.
[22] Ephesians 4:8-16.
[23] *Testimonies to Ministers,* pp. 26-29.
[24] Ephesians 4:17.
[25] Revelation 19:7.
[26] *Testimonies for the Church,* Vol. 9, p. 19.
[27] *Selected Messages,* Book Two, p. 390.
[28] Letter to D. M. Canright, *Testimonies for the Church,* Vol. 5, p. 571.
[29] *Selected Messages,* Book Two, p. 380.
[30] *Ibid.,* p. 397.
[31] Revelation 3:19.
[32] Vs. 21.
[33] Jeremiah 3:22.
[34] Psalm 121:4.
[35] *Selected Messages,* Book Two, p. 390.
[36] Revelation 3:21.
[37] 1 John 4:18.
[38] Zechariah 12:8.
[39] *Selected Messages,* Book Two, p. 71.
[40] *Review and Herald,* October 13, 1904.
[41] Romans 4:17.
[42] Daniel 8:14; cf. Revelation 11:15; 19:7, 8.
[43] *Review and Herald,* January 28, 1890.
[44] *Ibid.,* April 8, 1890.
[45] *Ibid.,* January 21, 1890.

$\mathcal{A}ppendix$

ELLEN G. WHITE ENDORSEMENTS
OF THE MESSAGE OF JONES AND WAGGONER

Footnote 6, Chapter Four, page 43:

The reader can find these and many other Ellen White endorsements of the message of Jones and Waggoner in the following sources (all are published in the four-volume *The Ellen G. White 1888 Materials*, and can easily be located by consulting the index in Volume 1):

• *Testimonies to Ministers,* pp. 70-80, 89-98, 410, 412, 413, 466, 467, 468.

• MSS 8a, 9, 13, 15, 21, 24, 1888.

• MSS 5, 10, 13, 30, 1889.

• Diary, April 7, 1889.

• Letter B-24, 1889.

• Letter W-1, 1889.

• Letters 30, 55, 1890.

• *Review and Herald,* February 12, July 23, 1889; March 18, May 27, 1890.

• Letter W-4, 1890.

• *General Conference Bulletin,* 1891, pp. 256-258, 260.

• Letters 19d, 1892; S-24, 1892; 25b, 1892; B2a, 1892; 25b, 1892; K-18, 1892; Letter January 9, 1893; Letter H-27, 1894; Letter 51a, 1895; Letter 96, 1896 (*Selected Messages,* Book One, pp . 234, 235).

The total number of Ellen White endorsements of the Jones Waggoner message runs above 370. Sometimes there are five or six on one page.

One endorsement from her inspired pen should be sufficient to motivate us to re-study the 1888 message. Two would emphasize its importance; three would make the matter urgent. But there are *hundreds* of enthusiastic endorsements, which must constitute the most emphatic call from a prophet that God's people have ever received in all time.

Index

FOR MORE ABOUT THE "MOST PRECIOUS MESSAGE"...

THE GLAD TIDINGS: GALATIANS MADE
CLEAR *by E. J. Waggoner*

The book that sparked the current revival of interest in the 1888 message. This verse-by-verse study of Paul's epistle to the Galatians was originally published in 1900, but it never loses its impact. Waggoner's stupendous vision of the cross of Christ is relevant present truth. Excellent for personal and group study. Six chapters, 144 pp. [00113]. Also available in Spanish [02101].

WAGGONER ON ROMANS: THE GOSPEL IN
PAUL'S GREAT LETTER *by E. J. Waggoner*

A companion book to *The Glad Tidings,* this verse-by-verse study of Romans was printed in *Signs of the Times* in 1895-96. In 1889-90 Ellen G. White said, "Let us have all of Romans and all of Galatians." Sixteen chapters, plus an appendix in question-and-answer format; 226 pp. [00140].

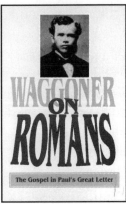

THE CONSECRATED WAY TO CHRISTIAN
PERFECTION *by A. T. Jones*

Jones presents Christ our Savior in the three offices of prophet, priest, and king, and focuses on His high priestly ministry in the heavenly sanctuary. Relates justification by faith to the unique Adventist idea of the cleansing of the sanctuary. Seventeen chapters, 92 pp. [00210].

CHRIST AND HIS RIGHTEOUSNESS by E. J. Waggoner

Waggoner penetrates centuries of spiritual fog to rediscover the inherent power of pure New Testament justification by faith. He puts his finger on the true reason for our many spiritual defeats—*unbelief*. But he brings spiritual sunshine to the reader by demonstrating how to overcome that sinful paralysis—by *believing* how good the Good News is. Enhanced with the addition of 14 more chapters, mainly from *Signs of the Times* on the same topic. 200 pp. [00150]. Also available in Spanish [02102].

1888 RE-EXAMINED by Robert J. Wieland and Donald K. Short

Seventh-day Adventists should know their fateful church history as presented in this landmark book. The 1888 General Conference Session and the tragic results are carefully delineated, showing that the "most precious message" was resisted and in a great measure rejected. Here Ellen White bears uninhibited testimony of what really happened in 1888, and the true reason for Christ's continuing delay. Prepared in 1950 as a private manuscript, this key document has since stirred Adventist hearts worldwide. Fifteen chapters, five appendices, and index; 243 pp. [00101].

LET HISTORY SPEAK compiled by Donald K. Short

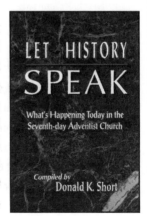

Now it can be told! For five years, by appointment of the General Conference officers, the Primacy of the Gospel Committee met behind closed doors. What happened? This book brings to the Seventh-day Adventist Church the startling witness of its history, past and present, showing how the Lord's plans for His people have been put on hold for over a century. This collection of documents presented to the Primacy of the Gospel Committee explores hidden reasons behind the apathy and widespread indifference that perplex sincere church members. Six papers, appendixes; 152 pp. [00154].

Further Reading from the Author of *Grace on Trial*

Robert J. Wieland has served his church as an ordained minister for nearly 50 years, 24 of which were in East Africa. A missionary and widely read author, he has stimulated renewed study of the fascinating message of 1888 as "present truth"—soul-winning Good News that heals the disease of lukewarmness.

THE 1888 MESSAGE: AN INTRODUCTION

Much has been published by the official Adventist press *about* "1888," But this book has a special purpose. It allows the 1888 messengers, Alonzo T. Jones and Ellet J. Waggoner, to tell what the message was (and is)—in their own words. The author demonstrates that the message of 1888 is not merely a "doctrine," but a living, vital experience based on doctrine, with relevance in today's world. The reader will find hope and encouragement. Sixteen chapters, appendixes, and indexes; 192 pp. [00138]. Also available in Spanish [02105].

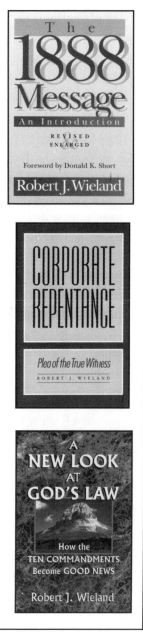

CORPORATE REPENTANCE: PLEA OF THE TRUE WITNESS

Deeper study into an intriguing subject, seldom understood. The meaning of the term "corporate repentance" is made crystal clear. It is the Lord Jesus Christ Himself who calls the Seventh-day Adventist Church leadership to corporate and denominational repentance. This book demonstrates both the possibility and certainty of an ultimate favorable response. 163 pp. [00110].

A NEW LOOK AT GOD'S LAW: HOW THE TEN COMMANDMENTS BECOME GOOD NEWS

A book that contains the best news anyone could read—God's stern Ten Commandments suddenly become Good News! Believe that "I am the Lord your God who has *already* brought you ... out of the house of bondage," and His Ten Commandments metamorphose before your eyes into assurance of blessings. 100 pp. [00151].

IN SEARCH OF THE CROSS: LEARNING TO "GLORY" IN IT

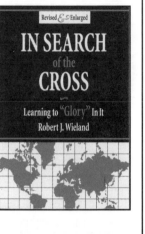

A joyous journey of discovery. Travel along with the author as he explores the journeys of those who have taken the road to the cross: Jesus, Mary Magdalene, and Paul. Published over and over, and in several languages, *In Search of the Cross* has stirred the pulse of readers on almost all continents. This is a touching and compelling book. 139 pp. [00149].

POWERFUL GOOD NEWS

Describes how a paralyzing counterfeit has been injected like a drug into our modern concepts of the simple message that should still be "the power of God to salvation." Spiritual frustration, depression, back-sliding—all are seen as a failure to perceive how good the Good News is. The Bible-based concepts set forth here will stir the reader like a breath of fresh air. Reviewed with enthiusiam in the *Adventist Review* of June 2001. 143 pp. [00125]. Also available as an AudioBook (four cassettes) read by the author [20202].

Glad Tidings Publishers
8784 Valley View Drive
Berrien Springs, MI 49103 U.S.A.
Order line: (616) 473-1888 • Fax: (616) 473-5851